Drug Abuse

Other books in the Social Issues Firsthand series:

Drug Abuse

Justin Karr, Book Editor

GREENHAVEN PRESS

An imprint of Thomson Gale, a part of The Thomson Corporation

Detroit • New York • San Francisco • New Haven, Conn. • Waterville, Maine • London

Christine Nasso, *Publisher*
Elizabeth Des Chenes, *Managing Editor*

© 2007 The Gale Group.

Star logo is a trademark and Gale and Greenhaven Press are registered trademarks used herein under license.

For more information, contact:
Greenhaven Press
27500 Drake Rd.
Farmington Hills, MI 48331-3535
Or you can visit our Internet site at http://www.gale.com

Articles in Greenhaven Press anthologies are often edited for length to meet page requirements. In addition, original titles of these works are changed to clearly present the main thesis and to explicitly indicate the author's opinion. Every effort is made to ensure that Greenhaven Press accurately reflects the original intent of the authors. Every effort has been made to trace the owners of copyrighted material.

Cover photograph reproduced by permission of Gstar.

LIBRARY OF CONGRESS CATALOGING-IN-PUBLICATION DATA

Drug abuse / Justin Karr, book editor.
   p. cm. -- (Social issues firsthand)
  Includes bibliographical references and index.
  ISBN-13: 978-0-7377-3838-4 (hardcover)
  1. Teenagers--Drug use. 2. Drug abuse. 3. Drug addicts. 4. Drug addicts--Rehabilitation. I. Karr, Justin.
  HV5724.Y68D78 2008
  613.8--dc22
                                     2007025679

ISBN-10: 0-7377-3838-3 (hardcover)

Printed in the United States of America
10 9 8 7 6 5 4 3 2 1

Contents

Chapter 3: Recovery

Chapter 4: Parental Views on Drug Abuse

Foreword

Social issues are often viewed in abstract terms. Pressing challenges such as poverty, homelessness, and addiction are viewed as problems to be defined and solved. Politicians, social scientists, and other experts engage in debates about the extent of the problems, their causes, and how best to remedy them. Often overlooked in these discussions is the human dimension of the issue. Behind every policy debate over poverty, homelessness, and substance abuse, for example, are real people struggling to make ends meet, to survive life on the streets, and to overcome addiction to drugs and alcohol. Their stories are ubiquitous and compelling. They are the stories of everyday people—perhaps your own family members or friends—and yet they rarely influence the debates taking place in state capitols, the national Congress, or the courts.

The disparity between the public debate and private experience of social issues is well illustrated by looking at the topic of poverty. Each year the U.S. Census Bureau establishes a poverty threshold. A household with an income below the threshold is defined as poor, while a household with an income above the threshold is considered able to live on a basic subsistence level. For example, in 2003 a family of two was considered poor if its income was less than $12,015; a family of four was defined as poor if its income was less than $18,810. Based on this system, the bureau estimates that 35.9 million Americans (12.5 percent of the population) lived below the poverty line in 2003, including 12.9 million children below the age of eighteen.

Commentators disagree about what these statistics mean. Social activists insist that the huge number of officially poor Americans translates into human suffering. Even many families that have incomes above the threshold, they maintain, are likely to be struggling to get by. Other commentators insist that the statistics exaggerate the problem of poverty in the United States. Compared to people in developing countries, they point out, most so-called poor families have a high quality of life. As stated by journalist Fidelis Iyebote, "Cars are owned by 70 percent of 'poor' households. . . . Color televisions belong to 97 percent of the 'poor' [and] videocassette recorders belong to nearly 75 percent. . . . Sixty-four percent have microwave ovens, half own a stereo system, and over a quarter possess an automatic dishwasher."

However, this debate over the poverty threshold and what it means is likely irrelevant to a person living in poverty. Simply put, poor people do not need the government to tell them whether they are poor. They can see it in the stack of bills they cannot pay. They are aware of it when they are forced to choose between paying rent or buying food for their children. They become painfully conscious of it when they lose their homes and are forced to live in their cars or on the streets. Indeed, the written stories of poor people define the meaning of poverty more vividly than a government bureaucracy could ever hope to. Narratives composed by the poor describe losing jobs due to injury or mental illness, depict horrific tales of childhood abuse and spousal violence, recount the loss of friends and family members. They evoke the slipping away of social supports and government assistance, the descent into substance abuse and addiction, the harsh realities of life on the streets. These are the perspectives on poverty that are too often omitted from discussions over the extent of the problem and how to solve it.

Greenhaven Press's Social Issues Firsthand series provides a forum for the often-overlooked human perspectives on society's most divisive topics of debate. Each volume focuses on one social issue and presents a collection of ten to sixteen narratives by those who have had personal involvement with the topic. Extra care has been taken to include a diverse range of perspectives. For example, in the volume on adoption, readers will find the stories of birth parents who have made an adoption plan, adoptive parents, and adoptees themselves. After exposure to these varied points of view, the reader will have a clearer understanding that adoption is an intense, emotional experience full of joyous highs and painful lows for all concerned.

The debate surrounding embryonic stem cell research illustrates the moral and ethical pressure that the public brings to bear on the scientific community. However, while nonexperts often criticize scientists for not considering the potential negative impact of their work, ironically the public's reaction against such discoveries can produce harmful results as well. For example, although the outcry against embryonic stem cell research in the United States has resulted in fewer embryos being destroyed, those with Parkinson's, such as actor Michael J. Fox, have argued that prohibiting the development of new stem cell lines ultimately will prevent a timely cure for the disease that is killing Fox and thousands of others.

Each book in the series contains several features that enhance its usefulness, including an in-depth introduction, an annotated table of contents, bibliographies for further research, a list of organizations to contact, and a thorough index. These elements—combined with the poignant voices of people touched by tragedy and triumph—make the Social Issues Firsthand series a valuable resource for research on today's topics of political discussion.

Introduction

Drug addiction is a complex disorder, and many people hold differing beliefs about the features and mechanics of the disorder. Definitions that are common knowledge in today's society, however, do not accurately correspond with the latest scientific and medical information on addiction, according to some members of the scientific and medical communities. Some scholars have argued that these conflicting definitions have had serious social consequences in the form of unreliable treatment programs, cost-prohibitive political policies with ambiguous results, and great suffering among addicts and those patients who benefit from the prolonged use of narcotics.

Models of Drug Addiction

The most widely known definitions of addiction are represented by the moral model, the exposure model, and the disease model. These definitions are taught in schools and held by the U.S. Drug Enforcement Administration (DEA), hospitals, law enforcement, parents, physicians, and others. The moral model purports that drug dependence is the result of poor character and bad personal choices arising from antisocial or irreligious attitudes. According to this model, the narcotics user starts abusing drugs out of malice or weakness in the face of "bad influences" and eventually becomes hopelessly addicted. The moral model has been thoroughly discarded by the medical and scientific communities. Research has shown that persons of "good character" or religious backgrounds, as well as socially active people, abuse drugs in the same proportions as other people. Likewise, many people considered asocial, irreligious, or of "poor character" do not use drugs at all. In addition, notions of character, antisocial behavior, and religion are not agreed upon by all people. One person's irreligious behavior, for instance, might be another person's spiritual awakening.

The exposure model, the underlying assumption of which forms the basis for the DEA's War on Drugs initiative, asserts that addiction is inevitable if one takes drugs for a long enough time and in sufficient quantities to become physically dependent on the substance. According to the DEA, addicts are "habitual" narcotics users who "have lost the power of self-control with reference to [their] addiction" or whose use "endangers the public morals, health, safety, or welfare." Such drugs as crack cocaine and heroin, according to the exposure theory, are themselves the cause of addiction; in other words, anyone who abuses these drugs will become addicted.

The disease model, which is the basis of hospital treatments, is described by such sources as the American Psychiatric Association's *Diagnostic and Statistical Manual of Mental Illnesses (DSM)* and the World Health Organization's *International Classification of Diseases (ICD)*. According to the *DSM*, addiction is "A maladaptive pattern of drug use, leading to impairment or distress." An addict is someone who shows three or more of the following symptoms during a year: tolerance to a drug; withdrawal; use of more drugs than intended; inability to control drug use; efforts to obtain a drug; replacement of important activities with drug use; and/or continued use despite negative consequences, including legal, health, and social problems.

The *ICD* refers to addiction as a "dependence syndrome" that consists of a number of mental and physical symptoms of drug use, notably "a strong desire to take the drug, difficulties in controlling its use, persisting in its use despite harmful consequences, a higher priority given to drug use than to other activities and obligations, increased tolerance, and sometimes a physical withdrawal state." Both the *ICD* and the *DSM* definitions emphasize negative consequences as indicators of drug addiction, but they also bear some similarity to the exposure model. The *DSM* lists tolerance, withdrawal, and efforts to obtain a drug as indicators of addiction, and the *ICD* maintains that symptoms appear after repeated use.

What Causes Addiction?

Doctors, scientists, and patient advocates who disagree with these definitions argue that some drugs are known to produce physical dependence, yet do not produce destructive craving, such as the antidepressant Prozac. Studies reported in the journal *Pain* (1982) and the *Journal of Pain and Symptom Management* (1992) have shown that even such opioids (natural or synthetic derivatives of opium) as Oxycontin and Oxycodone do not cause craving when used by chronic-pain and burn-unit patients to treat severe pain. Correspondingly, some doctors and scientists have argued that rather than destroying these patients' lives, such drugs enable them to function better, even at high doses that might kill an inexperienced user.

Several commentators have noted that recent studies of addiction have produced surprising results. For example, statistics concerning patterns of narcotics use in people who have taken drugs over a long period disprove some widely held views about drug abuse and addiction. The studies demonstrate that dependence on habit-forming substances such as crack cocaine, while widespread among people with a history of poverty or mental illness, is a rather rare phenomenon limited to about 5 percent of the total number of drug users. Furthermore, some steady drug users—notably chronic pain sufferers using opioids—who may be physically dependent on drugs, do not exhibit cravings or negative consequences due to drug use. Most of this research has come forth since the 1980s, and it has been generally accepted and duplicated by scientists who study addiction.

There are many unproven theories about how addiction happens, but some researchers have concluded that simply taking a drug on a regular basis, even daily, does not predict dependence, nor does the presence of withdrawal symptoms necessarily reflect addiction. Thus, they have argued, drugs themselves do not cause addiction. Rather, such factors as poverty and mental illnesses such as depression and bipolar disorder have been posited as precursors to addiction. A 1990 study found that emotional problems predisposed adolescents to heavy drug use. One particularly interesting theory, advanced by Canadian psychology professor Bruce K. Alexander, suggests that it is not drugs that cause addiction, but rather dislocation from traditional social ties (such as when workers have to move away from home to obtain employment) that leads to addictive behavior. According to Alexander, people succumb to addiction because they have no other options open to them to relieve the effects of displacement.

The Evolving Definition of Addiction

What really causes addiction? No one knows for sure, but some scientists have proposed that drugs themselves, even those that cause withdrawal, do not inevitably trigger addiction. They have also posited that dependence can be temporary and reversible. In fact, recent studies have revealed that drug users who escalate to addictive behavior are often able to break the pattern of harmful use without medical intervention or support groups. Doctors, community leaders, educators, and parents agree that addiction has terrible consequences, and unfortunately seems to most frequently affect those who can least afford its devastating effects—the poor, the mentally ill, and others who feel trapped by their circumstances. Some scholars have observed that addiction most commonly occurs in people who feel they have no recourse other than drug use to relieve their problems. Thus, to some in the scientific community, the commonly held definitions of addiction do not fully reflect the outcome of their most current research, which has suggested that emotional problems are the most reliable predictors of addiction. Others have argued that because of the complexity of the disease, no single factor can predict who will become an addict.

Given the lack of consensus in scholarly literature on what defines and causes drug addiction, research into the risk factors that lead to drug abuse is ongoing. Recent studies have begun to uncover the genes that contribute to a person's susceptibility to addiction, those that may protect a person from dependency, and the interaction between one's genetic makeup and one's environment. Specifically, such environmental factors as inadequate parent-child relationships and physical or sexual abuse, as well as internal factors including emotional and mental problems, have been acknowledged as precursors to addiction. As Nora D. Volkow of the National Institute on Drug Abuse summarized, "In the past 30 years, advances in science have revolutionized our understanding of drug abuse and drug addiction. Drug addiction is a brain disease." Scholars are continually publishing new findings about the workings of the human brain and the underlying sources and symptoms of dependency. Consequently, health-care professionals, government officials, teachers, and parents can begin to treat and prevent drug addiction with increased effectiveness.

SOCIAL ISSUES
FIRSTHAND

Teenagers and Drugs

Marijuana Behind the Wheel

Amanda B., as told to John DiConsiglio

Driving while under the influence of drugs is a growing problem among teens. Marijuana adversely affects a driver's peripheral vision, ability to focus, depth perception, and reaction time, resulting in disorientation and misjudgment behind the wheel. In the following selection, Amanda B. describes how her irresponsible choice to drive a car after getting high could have killed someone. A high school senior in 2006, the teen from Detroit, Michigan, has kicked her drug habit and turned her life around.

When I drove the car into the first garbage can, I giggled. "Ten points," I said. Then I hit another can. Everyone in the car laughed. I was driving—well, swerving, really—in my girlfriend's maroon Lumina. I aimed at a garbage can and hit the gas. Then I slammed on the brakes and drove slowly. Very slowly, maybe 10 miles an hour. Behind me, cars honked and flashed their lights. But I didn't care. My friends and I just laughed louder, and I veered all over the road. It was hard to see. The car was filled with smoke. And, besides, I'd forgotten to turn on the headlights.

But what did I care? I was 15 and high on marijuana.

I'm 17 now. And I haven't used pot—or any other drug—in almost a year. But since I first tried marijuana at 14, I smoked it on a daily basis. There are a lot of things about smoking marijuana that I regret. I failed most of my classes and ruined my reputation as a good student—and a good kid. My parents' trust in me vanished. I lost interest in everything I used to love, like going to art museums and making jewelry. Worst of all, it led me to experiment with other drugs like heroin.

Dangerous Driving

Right near the top of my list of regrets is getting high and getting behind the wheel of a car. I totaled my car three times in three months while driving high. I rear-ended dozens of other drivers. I fell asleep while driving my mom's car and hit a bunch of pylons, dragging them down the road and ruining the car's undercarriage. Once I passed out while driving my Oldsmobile in the middle of Detroit. When I woke up, I was doing a "lawn job"—circling around the grass of a stranger's yard. I hit a street sign and lost my front tooth. I ended up in the emergency room with a cap on my tooth and back pain that still won't go away. But it could have been much worse. I could have killed myself—or someone else.

You hear about drunk driving. But people don't talk as much about driving while smoking pot. Maybe it's because marijuana seems to be everywhere. It's easier for a teenager to get pot than beer. Even at 14, I could get it from a junior or senior at my high school. It was at every party. Sometimes my friends and I smoked it in our cars. We'd roll up the windows to keep the smoke in. We called it "clambaking"—sitting in a car filled with pot smoke, getting higher and higher.

Driving while high seemed like no big deal to me. Sometimes, I thought I drove even better when I was stoned. I convinced myself that the drug made me drive slower and pay more attention. But, of course, I was always speeding—or barely moving. Sometimes, I'd feel so relaxed that I'd fall asleep on the highway. I'd leave my lights on all day and burn out the car's battery or forget to turn them on when I drove at night. Once, a cop pulled my girlfriend and me over. He had followed us for a mile because our lights were off. He let us go with a warning. He couldn't tell we were stoned. And I just giggled and giggled. It always seemed funny to me when I was high.

Getting Help

After I went to the ER, my parents got me into rehab. They sent me to the Pathway Family Center, a drug-treatment facility for teens in Michigan. I've turned my life around. I'm back in school and getting better grades. My teachers are amazed. My relationship with my parents is good again. I'm even looking forward to going to college next fall. I want to be a kindergarten teacher like my mom.

But I still think about those nights when the pot smoke filled my girlfriend's Lumina. The car was always in bad shape. We'd already scratched the paint. The side view mirrors were ripped off from sideswiping other cars. I'd sit behind the wheel with a joint, pretending I was inside my own personal video game. It was like Mario Land. Ten points for crashing into a garbage can. Twenty for knocking down a mailbox. We'd giggle as the wheels slipped on the ice. It was one big party on wheels. If you saw us out on the road those nights, well, I hope you kept your distance. It might have saved your life.

Peer Pressure Leads to Drug Abuse

Natalie Porter

Peer pressure about drugs does not always come from bullies and scruffy-looking dealers. It comes in many different shapes and sizes. Natalie Porter, who began using drugs at age sixteen and quit five years later, describes how drugs and alcohol came to her in the hands of a friend.

Before I was 16, the words 'peer pressure' mustered visions of playground bullies surrounding their victim and forcing them to do something they didn't want to do. Peer pressure seemed so forceful, that I was sure I would see it coming. In my fantasies I would stand up to the bullies, confidently tell them, 'No I will not do what you tell me to do,' and stick to my guns.

If only it had been that simple, I might not have lost a good five years of my life. But peer pressure came to me in the shape of my friend, someone I trusted and respected.

My friend gave me a call out of the blue one day. We hadn't spoken for some years. I was 16, had just left school, was two weeks away from starting college and was feeling emotional, heart-broken and at a loose end after splitting up with my 'summer boyfriend.' She asked me what my plans for Saturday night were. I told her not much and she invited me to stay.

"Your Mother Need Not Know"

On Saturday night she said that we were going to her boyfriend's house and then on to a nightclub. 'Nightclub? My mother will kill me,' I said. She laughed and said, 'Your mother need not know.' That was the beginning of what was to become a follow-the-leader friendship.

Her boyfriend and his friends turned out to be quite a lot older. I felt a little intimidated by them, but as the night progressed I seemed to fit into their group and it felt good to belong and be accepted.

After about an hour at the nightclub, I noticed they were all taking ecstasy tablets. When they saw I had seen them, they smiled over at me and gestured did I want one. I shook my head. I felt sick all of a sudden, scared and alone and alienated. As I turned away, there was my friend. She smiled and said, 'Here, take this if you like. It's half an ecstasy. You don't have to worry about paying for it.'

"You're Our Friend Now"

I shook my head again. But I felt embarrassed and not so confident. I didn't want to be different, I wanted to fit in. "It's OK, you know," she said, "nothing will happen to you. We're all here to look after you, you're our friend now." A couple of them walked over casually and said, "Yeah, we think you're cool, Nat."

So much for the bullies surrounding their victim and being forceful. This was far more subtle. I felt obliged to share the tablet with my friend, because I didn't want to be the odd one out. As a teenager I was riddled with insecurities of non-belonging and loneliness. I only saw two possibilities, do this tablet and be accepted, or don't and be rejected.

And that was it. Every weekend we all went out together and used drugs. Over the next five years my friends offered me harder and harder drugs with higher and higher prices. I was as dependent on them as they were on me. We were a gang and needed each other in a very dangerous way. I left college, my relations with my parents failed, and I couldn't hold a job for longer than a month.

The drug dealer turned out not to be the dodgy looking guy on the street corner with the tatty clothes and unshaven face that my mother had told me about. He came in the shape of my friend, well-dressed, full of smiles and confidence.

Settled for Less

Not once did these new friends look after me as they had promised that night. Quite the contrary. Many times they abandoned me and left me in unfamiliar places with unknown people. Often they would take my last pound for drugs, leaving me with no money to get home safely. We all have standards about what we believe to be true friendship, but somewhere along the line I settled for less.

How did I get out of it? I was lucky: I had the chance of a lifetime, to go to Australia to take part in a course run by MRA [Moral Re-Armament, an organization dedicated to moral and spirtual renewal].

By then I had reached such a level of desperation that I was looking for ways out. But after years of drug and alcohol abuse I felt extremely weak in my will power, and didn't have the support network around me to help me break free.

When the chance came to go to Australia, it was a big decision to make. I had to take a harsh look at my life, which hurt, and decide to leave all that I had come to know—friends lifestyle, habits, behavioural patterns. I had to start my life again, without my old peer group.

Doing the Right Thing

I felt very alone but I knew that what I was doing was the right thing, long term. I needed time to go back to basics and to find what I had been lacking for the past five years—direction for my life and a faith, something to hold me through moments of aloneness. The first three months were the worst, because there was this uncertainty about whether I really wanted to leave the old life behind—wasn't there some way I could have the best of both worlds? There were times when I felt very homesick, but I soon realized that complete cut-off was the only way I could succeed.

During my time in Australia I learnt an alternative lifestyle, which was far more rewarding and fulfilling and which enabled me to repair the broken relations with my family. Now I have returned home, and have not returned to my old friends.

Do I regret my choices? No, not even the bad ones. They led me to a journey of self-discovery, of who I am and what my needs are. Breaking with the old peer group was hard at the time, but I spare them little thought now. It was time to move on. The past is the past and tomorrow is the future. But today is a gift, that's why it's called the present.

Addicted to Drugs at Age 13

Nick Shreve, as told to Alison Delsite Everett

Nick Shreve, aged seventeen in 2005, began smoking marijuana as a thirteen-year-old while growing up in Wellsburg, West Virginia, and soon progressed to crack cocaine and alcohol. He recounts his descent into addiction, noting that his drug use allowed him to ignore incidents that should have served as "wake-up calls" to him.

I was almost 13 years old and out fishing with some friends. I was having one of the best times of my life. One of the kids, who was 16, took out a joint, lit it and handed it to me. My lips pressed around the tip of it, and my lungs filled with smoke. I coughed but took another hit. That's when my life with drugs started.

I Am a Drug Addict

My name is Nick Shreve, and I'm 17. I live in Wellsburg [West Virginia] with my parents, three brothers and sister.

I am a drug addict. I am telling my story because I hope it will spare another kid from the hell I've been through and have put my family through.

I won't lie—when I took a hit while fishing that day, I liked the way it made me feel. From that day on, I started smoking marijuana whenever I could. When my parents would give me $20, instead of spending the money on movies or at the mall, I'd buy a bag of weed.

A year later, dad was working 45 miles away in Pittsburgh [Pennsylvania]. I begged my mom to let me stay with him during the week and go to school there. I thought it would be more interesting than life in my small town.

Nick Shreve, as told to Alison Delsite Everett, "Drugs Are Not the Answer," *Boys' Life*, vol. 95, no. 11, November 2005, pp. 46–51. Reproduced by permission.

I loved living with my dad because he was working. I met a kid who sold drugs, and he become my only friend while I was there. One day, he sold me $20 of crack. Soon, I was smoking crack nearly every day, never thinking about what I was doing to myself. I didn't even realize that already I was an addict.

One day, I couldn't find my friend, and I was desperate to get high. I walked up the street to a hardware store and bought a can of compressed air. I went to my room, put the can to my mouth and took a deep breath. When I awoke, my mom was standing over me, crying and looking scared. She thought I was dead. She said I was shaking, convulsing, and that there was white foam coming from my mouth. I promised her it was the first—and last—time I ever did that. You would think that would have been a wake-up call for me, but it wasn't. I just smoked more crack and weed.

My Life Was Getting Out of Control

The summer I was still 13, two friends and I were fooling around and made three homemade bombs. We weren't out to hurt anyone. We threw them into a neighbor's yard and state police were called. I was arrested and sentenced to 90 days at George Junior Republic, a juvenile detention program.

Before I left for George Junior, one of my best friends was killed. She was a great girl, got good grades, graduated from high school early and was going to college to study to be a lawyer. She was going to do something with her life. She had been popping pills that day and was driving too fast and smashed into a tree. That should have been another wake-up call for me.

I just did more and more drugs to hide the pain.

I Hated My Life

I learned a lot about myself at George Junior. I found out what a good person I am when I'm not using drugs. As the drugs came out of my system, I was happier with myself, and others seemed happier with me.

After I came back from George Junior, I stayed clean for about four months. One of my good friends, Andrew, was having problems at home and was staying with my family once in a while. Andrew went down to the river to party with two friends one summer afternoon. They were drinking, getting high and doing pills. Andrew was in the water and went under. His two friends were afraid they would get busted for the beer and drugs, so they took off. They left Andrew in the water.

Two days later the police pulled Andrew's body from the river. That made me wonder about some of the people I called friends.

It Should Have Been Perfect

That fall, I started dating a girl and fell for her—hard. I was in love for the first time in my life. It should have been perfect. She wanted me to stop smoking so I wouldn't get sent away, but the addiction was too strong. I couldn't stop.

No one knew it, but by this time I was also smoking heroin. That's the thing about addiction. You start with one drug and it seems harmless, but before you realize it, you're doing harder drugs. My probation officer showed up at school one day to give me a drug test and said it was my last chance. I knew I was going to fail. I was in a haze most of that week, and my moods were swinging out of control. I wanted to run away from everything. One day, I drank a liter of grain alcohol. I blacked out and went kind of crazy. I smashed my head into a wall, threatened to kill myself, said horrible things to my parents and my girlfriend and didn't even notice how scared my little brothers were. When I leaped out of an upstairs window, my parents called the police. They took me to the emergency room, and from there I went to a youth mental hospital by order of the judge. I was there for about 10 days.

When I was released I was put on house arrest until my court hearing. I was certain that I'd be put away for six months or more. My mom found Gateway Rehabilitation Center, a drug and alcohol treatment center near Pittsburgh. I thank God that the judge sentenced me to 90 to 120 days there.

Ripping My Mom's Heart Out

The day I drove to Gateway—April 5, 2004—I could tell it was ripping my mom's heart out. Yet, she was relieved. She knew I'd be alive.

I hated my life. I hated everything. I didn't even realize how good I had it. My parents were really good to us, and I had everything a kid could want—video games, a $700 home theater system in my room.

Thing is, when you're an addict, drugs are all that matter to you.

Why Am I Still Here?

I am clean now. I still have urges to use drugs, but when that happens, I think, "That ain't cool," and I end up not doing it.

I'll always be an addict. I can't change that. But I'm working hard on being an addict in recovery instead of an addict who is using. I'm taking one day at time.

Often, I wonder why I'm still alive when so many others didn't make it this far or get this many chances.

My message: No matter how bad things get at home, no matter how bad things get at school, drugs are not the answer. They may make you feel better for a while, but after that, it's all downhill. Your life will just get worse.

Drug-Free and Proud

Leah Paulos

Teens Caitlin Lee and Colleen Grucella have chosen to lead drug-free lives. In the following selection, they discuss the factors that influenced their commitment to making smart choices about drug use regardless of peer pressure. Caitlin, who avoids drugs in part because she is a role model for her younger brother, attends Centennial High School in Peoria, Arizona. Colleen is a student at Penn Ridge High School in Sellersville, Pennsylvania, and cites her father's death from a drug overdose as her motivation to stay away from drugs. Leah Paulos is a writer, an editor, and a frequent contributor to Scholastic Choices.

The pressure to do drugs is always there for teenagers, but these days teen girls seem to really be feeling the heat. A recent study released by the White House Office of National Drug Control Policy says that teen girls have caught up with teen boys in illegal drug and alcohol use. To make matters worse, the study says that teen girls are more likely than their male peers to abuse prescription drugs and cigarettes.

But guess what? Not every teen is doing drugs. To prove that point, *Choices* interviewed two girls, Caitlin Lee and Colleen Grucella, about their decisions to stay substance-free, and about how exciting their lives are without drugs.

Caitlin's Story

Caitlin, a 15-year-old freshman at Centennial High School in Peoria, Arizona, doesn't have any desire to try drugs or alcohol. "I always hear stupid stories about things people do when they are high or out-of-control drunk," she tells *Choices*. "I recently saw a cross on the side of a road where five high school kids died from drunk driving. And I once heard on the news about a girl who walked into the street and got hit by a car while she was high."

The teen also hears scary stories from her parents: Caitlin's father, a police officer, told her about the time he arrested a guy on drugs who was trying to hold up a store with a butter knife. And some kids her mother teaches at a preschool have disabilities that were caused by their parents' drug use.

Caitlin says these kinds of stories help her stay drug-free. "Why would I want to do anything to hurt myself or someone else?" she asks.

Caitlin believes that teens start doing drugs to escape from some of the pressures they face, like fitting in at school, getting good grades, finding time to play on sports teams, and going to the cool parties. "Girls also get stressed about looking good and wearing the right clothes," Caitlin says. "Getting a pimple can ruin a whole week."

Stress Busters

Caitlin admits that she feels stress too, but says she deals with it in a more positive way. The teen is passionate about her hobbies, which include playing the flute and guitar. She is also a photographer.

Her social circle is a source of strength too. "I relax and enjoy myself by hanging out at the mall, having sleepover parties with my friends," Caitlin says. "We all help each other and listen to each other."

Caitlin admits that she's worried about facing more intense peer pressure to try drugs as she gets older. "But I am confident that I can stick to my beliefs," she says. "Every time I stick to my decision not to use drugs, my self-esteem gets stronger. I feel better about myself."

Caitlin wants to study journalism or psychology in college so she can help people. "I don't want to risk ruining my dreams by making a bad decision," she says. And finally, she has a sibling whom she doesn't want to let down. "I have a 7-year-old brother who looks up to me," Caitlin says. "I don't want him to look up to a drug user."

Colleen's Tale

Five years ago, Colleen got some news that changed her life forever. Her father, who had been struggling with a drug problem and had been in and out of rehab since he was a teen, died of a drug overdose. "He had so much to live for, but he couldn't see that fact because he was addicted to drugs," says Colleen, now a 17-year-old senior at Penn Ridge High School in Sellersville, Pennsylvania.

In high school, her dad had been a talented football player, but when he injured his knee he was so upset that he turned to drugs to help him cope. "He took a bad situation and made it so much worse," Colleen says. "What better proof do I need to see that drugs ruin lives?"

Some people might deal with a painful loss by turning to drugs and alcohol to help cope with the grief. Instead, Colleen makes it a point to stay away from drugs entirely. She is really proud of the fact that she has never tried them and plans never to try them. "How many high school students can say that?" Colleen asks. "I consider it a real accomplishment. It's a part of my identity now—I am someone who is drug-free!"

Fab Friends

She spends her free time playing basketball and hanging out with her friends and her boyfriend, none of whom do drugs. "We watch movies, go bowling, or go out to dinner and just laugh," Colleen says. "As long as I'm hanging out with friends, we have a great time."

Colleen isn't shy about sharing the story of what happened to her father with other teens. "If other people can learn from it, then I want to tell the story," she says. "Sometimes the dangers of drugs seem abstract or exaggerated, but I have a real story of what happened to a real person—my own dad—when he used drugs."

She adds that her dad, and others around him, always thought he would grow out of using drugs—that he would just abuse them as a teenager. Unfortunately, that did not happen.

"I don't want to go down that road," Colleen says. "There are a lot of things that make me happy in my life, like playing basketball and hanging out with my little brother. I don't want to jeopardize my future."

CHAPTER 2

Diary of a Drug User

My Life as a Narcotic Addict

David Herkt

In a world where the opportunities for adventure and testing one's strength and limits are shrinking daily, some people use drugs precisely because they are dangerous. David Herkt, a poet and educator concerned with HIV/AIDS, drugs, and drug use issues, recounts his day-to-day life as a heroin addict living in Australia and New Zealand and explains the fascination heroin has held for him.

Night-booted, walking along 3:00 A.M. Smith Street, that straight street, that great street, my feet knowing this very familiar route, up past the pharmacy where the pink and blue neon glows brightly on the dusty pavement and the sound of my boots comes in a set rhythm now to accompany my thoughts still amphetamine-propelled and soaring into the night above me.

I am walking home, walking up Smith Street towards Johnston, passing now the St Mark's Opportunity Shop, windows bleak with discarded objects whose sadness at this hour in their lonely arrangement is almost palpable, crossing over Otter Street towards the poster-covered windows of Sullivan's pawnbrokers, the pattern of the city suddenly shifting all around me as Otter Street gives a brief open view over Richmond, where each of the street lights possesses an iridescent halo in the faintly misty air and this grid array of sodium and halogen lamps hums in my mind with the same oiled static-scented sound that I associate with electric generators.

I push my hand into the front left-hand pocket of my black jeans to know the presence of a gram of amphetamine in its press-top plastic sachet, and, even more secret, even

David Herkt, "It Must Have Been a Terrible War," *Meanjin*, vol. 61, June 2002, pp. 105–116. Copyright © 1998–2006 *Meanjin*. Reproduced by permission of the author.

more precious to me, $75 worth of heroin in its small folded paper envelope, half of which I will use as soon as I reach my home. My fingertips slide over the plastic sachet and tenderly shape the paper of the small rectangle of the heroin. I am happy here, the sound of my boots on the dry pavement, the rhythm of my walk imposed on my thoughts, which spiral upwards in a tight screw of continuing motion that has almost no content now at the end of the long evening. I am pure speed at this moment, almost wordless, propelled forward from the coiled tension of the drug within, onward and outward. The warmth and darkness of the heroin I will inject when I reach my home is a sweet and solid anticipation now. My footsteps quicken. The electric night is all about me.

It Must All Be Endured

Huge fleshy white magnolia flowers rot amid their brass-green foliage in the humid air. I am at my parents' home in New Zealand. I am forty-one. I am withdrawing from my opiate dependency for the first time in ten years, and even then it was only a temporary phenomenon, let's say it is more like eighteen years. It is the second day of my withdrawal. I cannot get comfortable. At my wrist, elbows, knees and ankles, it feels as if knots of electricity have collected and must discharge themselves into jerking, flaring movement. I cannot lie still. Sleep is impossible. It is afternoon. I toss and turn and toss again on the single bed. The sheets are woven from some synthetic mix and the dry sharp quality of the material is uncomfortable. I find myself longing for my own cotton sheets. I am experiencing a strange chemical loneliness. Nothing comes from the outside to fill me. I long for a syringe part-filled with heroin but I also know I have set a situation into play that makes this impossible. I even long for the voices of familiar friends but they are all in another continent. I am hopelessly resigned. I twist my body, attempting to get comfortable in the strange humid air of a country where I have not lived for fifteen years. Sounds seem to echo and repeat in liquid profusion in the atmosphere. It must all be endured.

In the empty carpark below the deserted tennis courts there is only one car, a dull-coloured station wagon. 'He's here already' I say, 'don't park too close to him.' I am counting up a wad of cash. Each note must face the same way in the roll. He prefers this. There is $3000 here. It is an amount with which I am fully familiar. Each day I come out here with H—and we buy an ounce of heroin from M—for the same price. I have already done this once today. Now I am buying an ounce for someone else. I will profit from this transaction. Each ounce contains 28 grams of heroin. I will receive 2.8 grams of the drug, ten per cent, in return for my brokering services. The driver of the car is a young and unsuccessful architect. His girlfriend is a junky and she has talked him into buying a wholesale quantity of the drug by convincing him that he will be able to sell it through her and make a profit as well as supporting her own daily and his more casual use. I know this is unlikely. They will use too much. They will not recoup their investment. They will not be back.

He parks the car about twenty metres from the station wagon. I can recognise M—'s familiar silhouette behind the wheel of the other car. I roll up the money and put a rubber band around it. I keep rubber bands especially for this purpose. M—likes the money in a roll wrapped with a rubber band. I attempt to satisfy all his whims. He is, after all, the means by which I can support my heroin habit. He has not failed me in more than a year. I can buy any amount from him, whether it is $50 worth or $50,000. I am sure he likes me but I do not push my luck and I attempt to do things the way he likes them to be done. 'He's not going to rip us off?' asks the architect in what I consider to be a tedious display of nervousness. 'No,' I say attempting to reassure him, 'I see him every day. It's his business.' I get out of the car, the money in my pocket. Walking between the two cars I am suddenly aware of every metre of that space and the two pairs of eyes that watch me. I become conscious of the way I am walking. The day is a typical Melbourne summer's day. The sky is stark and blue, without cloud or wind and the heat has gathered and settled above the tarmac in that carpark. There is a row of gum trees above the carpark by the empty tennis courts. I go round to the passenger side of M—'s car and get in. It is all business now. We barely exchange glances. I pull the money out. 'It's all there,' I say. 'I've counted it.' He checks it anyway. As he counts he suddenly comes upon a note that has somehow been placed the wrong way. 'Sorry,' I say. He looks at me balefully then goes back to flicking over the fifty-dollar notes. When he is satisfied he reaches in under the dashboard and pulls out the ounce of heroin and hands it to me. I fold my hand around it and put it in my pocket. 'Okay,' I say, 'I'll see you tomorrow. Probably be around ten o'clock. We're having a busy day at home.' H— and I sell at least an ounce a day, split into deals, around eight deals per gram, at $50 a deal. We do not profit financially from this at all. We simply cover our own usage. If we sell more, we use more. 'I'll be home,' he replies, already reaching for the ignition.

I get out of the car and, while I am walking back to the architect, M—drives off. I get in the front seat and hand the ounce over to the architect. He looks at it. 'Did you check it?' he asks me, looking at the plastic bag which is still tightly closed with tape. 'It's OK,' I reply. 'Jesus,' he exclaims, 'You could have checked it.' I have to wait while he opens the package, dips his finger in the powder and tastes a little on his tongue. I hate the taste of heroin and if it is at all avoidable I don't taste it. 'It's OK,' he says with some relief. I just want to get back home now. H—will be pissed off having had to deal with the customers by herself and besides, I want to have a good big blast with some of the extra dope I have scored by brokering this transaction. 'Let's go then,' I say and he finally starts the car.

Regulating Consciousness with Drugs

Brown rocks. Pink rocks. White powder. The beige. Colours of consciousness.

Dusty sparrows are fidgeting in the vines that cover the brick walls of the back courtyard. Lying on a deckchair in the shade of the gnarled peach tree, I am nodding off. Metabolically I incline towards hyperactivity and so it is not often that I go on the nod. Frequently late at night, when I have visitors, I am the only person in the room still alert and fully conscious. At the moment I am trying to read a book but not succeeding. Every time I manage to read a line or so, my eyelids droop and my head relaxes. I am enjoying it. I have no pressing schedule today. I have more than enough heroin to last me until tomorrow. It is the weekend. I can hear distant lawnmowers. When I nod into the warm drowsy darkness, sudden vivid images flash into my mind. Invariably brief, these images interest me but like all unconscious dreaming it is hard to remember them. I nod again and I am suddenly presented with a view from the stem of a deep-sea game-fishing launch. Seagulls wheel in curves over the V-shaped foaming wake, which opens out towards the hazy horizon. I can see the two fishing rods at the stem quite clearly. Then as suddenly as it has come this image dissolves and I rouse my head and blink into the bright sunlight in the courtyard. Then sometime this afternoon, later on, still sitting in the green-and-orange-striped deckchair, I receive an image of a cool alpine lake in a calm almost mirror-like bowl between mountains, with a great huge red-hot iron grid suspended in the pale blue sky above it, stretching out an immense heavy length above this scene and glowing fiercely.

November 1995: A third of a gram of brittle methamphetamine crystals injected that morning upon waking at 7:00 A.M., the sudden launch of my body on that speed into my day and reading the *Age* and the *Australian* over my breakfast coffee and muesli. I like my morning newspapers. Then I have to walk to the chemist's. I am usually there early. So it is 70 mg [milligrams] of methadone at the pharmacy at 9:00 A.M. drunk in 15 ml [millileters] of sweetened gold-brown liquid and washed down with a glass of water, coming on slowly afterwards, smoothing out the speed, filling in the flesh. Then it is $75 worth of heroin at 11:00 A.M., injected, the whole-body stone now achieved and its clarity known, comfortable here, then my doctor friend gives me something and so it is one 2-ml vial of pethidine and one 1-ml vial of morphine, milligrams of active drug unrecalled, injected at 2:00 P.M., deepening the opiate-hold over my flesh, the long sunny hours, the shaded house, butterflies flickering in the garden, then another $75 worth of heroin at 5:00 P.M. injected because about now I am beginning to need another hit, another half gram of methamphetamine at 6.30 P.M., to set my thoughts moving on their wilful freeway, then settling down to the twilight and the deepening evening, Foster's lager in the fridge, carrying a blue can from room to room with me, and then finally four 10-mg Temazepam capsules emptied of their thick contents and injected slowly at about 1:00 A.M. to send me to sleep in the way that I have come to prefer, with a big darkening wave poised above and falling slowly down over my conscious mind.

With O—, and we are both hitting up in a toilet cubicle together, squeezed into that tight confine, our forearms bare, each of us concentrating on injecting the heroin we have just bought from R—'Mmm-mnn,' I say as the drug floods home, and then I raise my forearm to my mouth to suck off the small trickle of blood that has come from my injection site. I can taste iron and a small afterbitterness of the heroin. He is always faster than me. He is already capping his syringe. 'Makes it all worthwhile,' he comments, and we grin at each other there in that tile-lined cubicle.

Finding Tranquility in a Toilet Stall

My work that year involved lots of travel. Barely a week would pass without at least two plane trips. I was commuting between Melbourne and Canberra with frequency, then I was also required in Sydney at intervals as well as supervising two projects that were being conducted in Darwin. I was still enamoured with flying then. I loved the take-off procedure, from the moment the captain asked the crew to arm doors and cross-check, through the long taxi to the runway to the take off itself, the Boeing or the Airbus accelerating along the tarmac and then suddenly rising into the air. As soon as the seat-belt sign flashed off after the power turn, I would go to the toilet. Once behind the locked door, I would pull out all the necessary equipment, the new syringe and needle, the plastic ampoule of distilled water, a stainless steel spoon, alcohol swabs and the package of heroin. I would lay down the spoon by the small washbasin, swab it out, then put in the amount of the heroin I allowed myself, open the sterile water ampoule and the plastic wrapper of the syringe, take out some of the water up into the syringe, squeeze it back out over the heroin in the spoon, pull out the plunger of the syringe and stir the mix with it until the heroin dissolved. Then I put the plunger back, tore off a corner of a fresh alcohol swab to make a filter, put this in the mix, placed the syringe on it and drew the mix up through it, then flicked out any air-bubbles, used my shirtsleeve as a tourniquet, screwing it tightly round my upper arm, stretched my arm out before me and neatly injected myself.

There was something about hitting up eight kilometres above Australia, enclosed in the long silver cylinders of the aircraft that I loved so much. These were somehow complementary experiences; the sudden rush of the heroin in the blood like a great fast wave travelling over the body towards the bright brain, the sudden ease of the flesh and the clear transition of the mind to a state of tranquillity, and the movement of those planes through the rarefied air of those forever sunny heights. For a single sighing instant I would let myself relax there in that small toilet. I would then return to my seat and read or write, cool, calm and collected amid my fellow passengers, the hostesses moving down the aisle in slow motion with the drinks trolley and, through the cabin window, the pale-blue cloudless sky.

Bright cheap glitter of speed, chromium spaciousness of cocaine, subdued liquid gleams of heroin, darkening twilight of benzodiazepines, and the very, very black barbiturates.

'I'd Have Some Sort of Public Award by Now'

He overdosed. He often did. I had warned him. 'Don't have too much,' I had told him, 'because it's very strong.' He had reduced his amount, though not by enough, and when I turned around he had keeled over on the sofa, his lips already turning blue. It was very boring. His girlfriend began wailing. 'Shut up', I said. If she didn't shut up I would have had no compunction about slapping her. The whole thing was boring enough without having unwarranted hysteria. I must have sounded authoritative because she shut up. I walked over to him and stretched him out face up on the sofa.

His blue lips had drawn back from his teeth. I hated that. It reminded me of a photograph I had seen of the mummy of Rameses II. Looking at him I was reminded that I was about to battle with death for him. I took a deep breath and began to give him mouth-to-mouth. I began to kiss death then, breathing living air into this body that would die without my support. Within two breaths his lips began to turn pink again. At least his heart was still working. It takes a lot of heroin to give heart failure and usually respiration is the only thing you have to worry about. I pulled a cigarette out of a packet and lit it, looking around for an ashtray. 'Can you get me an ashtray?' I asked his girlfriend. She was still staring at him as his lips began to turn blue again. 'Ashtray', I said again. She got me the ashtray and I put my cigarette in it. Then I began to give him my breath again. It is a very intimate moment. No matter what your relationship is with the person who has overdosed, all of a sudden you are mouth-to-mouth with them and breathing your life into them. They call it the kiss of life and it's true. It is. I gave him a couple of breaths and took another drag on my cigarette. I had learned early on in my drug-using career not to panic. It was simply a matter of keeping them breathing until they can be revived. I guess if I added it up there were about twenty or thirty people who owed their lives to me for keeping them going after they had a heroin overdose. Sometimes I used to think that if I had been a surf-lifesaver instead of a junky I'd have some sort of public award by now. It took me forty minutes before I could revive him. I admit I was beginning to worry by then and I was even contemplating an ambulance but he came round. I slapped him on the face again after giving him three or four quick breaths in a row and he opened his eyes. 'Whattaya hitting me for?' he said. I didn't have much sympathy left at that stage so I didn't bother answering him. It's funny, but I have never overdosed in my whole drug-using career. I don't know what it is. It wasn't as if I didn't take risks or anything. I can remember a couple of times when I thought about overdosing. I never did though. Maybe it's just the metabolism you've got. Maybe it's the whole way you approach drug use. Who knows?. . .

'I Love Those Syringes'

I love syringes. I prefer the smaller 1-ml size, Terumo brand for preference, the small orange cap that covers the needle, the long slim transparent shaft with the marked gradations, the white plastic plunger. I will sometimes laughingly compare them to Benson & Hedges 100s, those slimline cigarettes one sees advertised in women's glossy magazines. These syringes are delicate to use and I am an expert in their handling. I can hit myself up in less than ten seconds. I am also frequently called upon to inject others. I am very good at it. But it is in the moments when I am alone, in a bathroom or the white-tiled toilet at work, or in my own bedroom, sitting on the edge of the double bed, that I love those syringes the most, their weightlessness in the fingers, their comfort in the slight grip one needs, their charm and airy ease as they perform the task for which they, were designed. . . .

Casual ease of conversation now. Before, when the five of us were waiting for the knock on the front door which meant that our heroin was being delivered, the conversation was tight with highpitched flights and nervous tension. Now everything is relaxed. The conversation flows upon easy lines, measured and comfortable. Someone is scratching their nose, I can hear the heroin in the husking voices about me. I am making a cup of tea for everyone. Outside the clear Australian dry sky is blue and deep. The old bricks of the North Carlton garden wall glow softly red. . . .

As I flew home from Darwin I was beginning to withdraw. The aircraft's air conditioning goosepimpled my skin. My thoughts were rushing pell-mell. I had already had that hour long sensual sleepy nap that marks, for me, the beginnings of withdrawal. I could now smell my own sweat. I was beginning to feel nauseous when I arrived in Canberra. On the way back home from the airport I made K—stop at five pharmacies.

I now have a substance I can mix and prepare. The whole process has taken me two hours and ten minutes. I go into the lounge room, sit at the table, fill a syringe with a bit of the now yellow liquid and inject it. The mixture hits my opiate-starved body like a sledgehammer. The imperfectly synthesised mixture contains codeine, morphine and heroin. The rush is nothing if not solid. It prickles with the remains of the codeine and morphine. I have enough to last me three days. It is very strong and a minute after having it I feel like I just want to sprawl on the couch and relax, but I've got to do the washing up.

Haunted by Heroin

Smell of heroin, it is strange but it does seem, in the face of impossibility, to have a smell that seems to percolate outwards, even into the surrounding streets, for I have had the experience of smelling it every time I walked past a certain house only to find myself months or years later scoring there, in that house, for the first time. I know this sounds impossible but it is true. Then the taste of the drug on the tongue and in the throat after injecting it. You put the syringe in your vein, inject the drug and then, as it hits, you can taste it in your mouth, a taste that is like high mountains, oxygen, faintly artificial but very clear, transparent and blue.

Dreaming of heroin, having packets of it or even a pile on a glass-topped coffee table, great huge syringes longer than in real life, mixing it up, or sitting in a locked strange bathroom with infinite white-tiled walls, or in some dark strange stairwell, trying to get this syringe into my arm. You never do in dreams. You never get that syringe into your arm. It's something junkies often comment about. You simply never get to hit up in dreams. You want it. How you want that dream-soft blow of the heroin to drift through your body. How you want to taste the drug on your tongue and the back of your throat the way you do when it is strong. How you want it. You are almost salivating with want. But you never get that syringe into your arm when you are dreaming. You never get to inject that dream drug. Sometimes you will get the needle into the vein but you always wake up before you can push the plunger. No such thing as a free lunch, I guess.

Why did I want to become a junkie? In the late twentieth century there were few frontiers. Go west, young man, they had said for a thousand years, the westward drift of European culture towards the Americas, the poor, the huddled masses in steerage, the Ellis Islands of welcome, the grassy prairies, the thick redwoods. All gone now. East met West a long time ago. Certainly there was upward, there was space, the final frontier, and we pushed the envelope towards the moon, lifted off by a Saturn rocket, the slow-motion movements of sucking a liquid lunch in an Apollo capsule accompanied on the sound system by lonesome steel guitars and Tammy Wynette's arms staying open late until you come home, but how many get to do this, huh? Not many. For the majority of mankind, there are no longer any physical frontiers. There are no free places, no imagined lands without the structures of corporate capitalism, no tropic islands where there is all the space one needs, where one can construct a life in accordance with one's desires, the desire for open horizons and ease of impulsive movement.

Now, the frontiers remain within oneself. So it was that I took drugs. Just as a legless man will use prosthetics to enable him to walk, so too did I take drugs to achieve freedom. By drug use I could extend myself outwards until I curved over the very edge of the earth, until my horizons were limitless. By my drug use I learned the reach and stretch of myself better than any other way I knew. In the absence of virgin prairies or the spinifex-dotted outback of beyond, I discovered the only new world left to me.

I Was Addicted to Crystal Meth

Nicole O'Bryan, as told to Cecelia Goodnow

Nicole O'Bryan, born in Boise, Idaho, in 1987, recalls how her life was disrupted by her family's move to Spokane, Washington. Seeking companionship in her strange new home, she got involved with a bad crowd, first smoking marijuana and then becoming addicted to crystal methamphetamine before her family helped her get into treatment.

I spent most of childhood in Boise, Idaho. It was a great place to grow up: Everyone knew each other, and I had tons of friends living nearby—I was always outside playing kickball and soccer on my street. But when I was 11, everything changed. One August day in 1998, my mom just said, "We're moving to Spokane, Washington." She'd gotten a good job there. I didn't want to leave all my friends, so I begged her to change her mind. But she wouldn't—and a month later, we left Boise for good. On our new street in Spokane, everything was totally different: Our neighbors didn't even try to be friendly. Sure, I met a couple of girls, but it just wasn't the same. I hated it there, so I spent most of my time at school or at home—wishing I was back in Boise.

First Taste

For the next three years. I just focused on school. But when I was 14, in July 2001. I met Kevin. I was out walking around with my neighbor, and we ran into this guy Jason we knew from school, and Kevin was with him. I'd never talked to Kevin before. All I knew about him was that he smoked a lot

Nicole O'Bryan, as told to Cecelia Goodnow, "I Was Addicted to Crystal Meth," *CosmoGIRL!*, vol. 6, no. 4, May 2004, pp. 120–21. Reproduced by permission of the author.

of pot. But that didn't bother me—I didn't really think pot was that big of a deal because lots of kids at school smoked. And I thought Kevin was really cute. We started dating about a week later.

Kevin didn't smoke pot around me at first. But one day, a couple of weeks after we started going out, he just asked me. "Want to go smoke?" I didn't want him to think I was a dork, so I went. We walked to the woods, where four of Kevin's friends were sitting on some rocks, passing around a pipe. I took a couple of hits of the pot, but I didn't feel any different—just really mature, because Kevin's friends were two years older, and I was sure they now thought I was cool. I never smoked with Kevin again after that—and we broke up like a month later.

In September, I started high school and met this girl Sarah in gym class. We became friends, and one day she took me to this guy's apartment, where a bunch of people I didn't know were hanging out. Everyone was smoking pot, so I tried it again. This time, I got really talkative—not shy at all, like I normally was. I was like the life of the party—and I wanted to feel that way all the time. Sarah and I started going downtown where the pot heads hung out to get high whenever we could. Soon I was smoking pot every day.

Downward Spiral

At first, getting high so much wasn't really a problem. I still did well in school, and my mom never found out about it. But in the fall of 2002, my sophomore year. I started skipping school to get high—and my grades quickly fell from A's to D's. My mom tried to talk to me about it, but I just refused to go to school—I'd tell her I was going but then I'd head downtown instead.

Later that school year, in March 2003, I met Connor, a cousin of this pothead I knew, and we started going out. Connor was 15 too, and he'd just moved to town. His family was pretty messed up—he lived in a hotel with his mom, who was addicted to painkillers and drank a lot. But he was the sweetest guy I'd ever met. He never said anything bad about anyone or got into fights. He was also a big pot smoker—so I got high with him. Soon his mom was giving him all kinds of drugs—pain pills, psychedelic mushrooms—and he was taking something pretty much every day. So that's what I started to do too.

A month after we started dating, Connor and I were at this park, and he started smoking crystal meth. I'd tried so many drugs by then. I didn't think twice when he passed me the pipe. But after I smoked, I got really restless, talking fast and pacing. We had a bonfire going, and all of a sudden, I got this urge to cut down some branches to feed the fire. I asked this guy for a knife and walked over to the trees and just started cutting like crazy. I was so determined—getting firewood seemed like the most important thing in the world at that moment. Then, out of the blue, I started to cry. And two seconds later, I was laughing hysterically, I had no control.

Connor started doing meth a lot—and by June, we were going on these four-day binges where all we'd do was smoke it. I didn't even like it that much, but when I *wasn't* on it, I'd get this horrible nauseous feeling with constant chills, so I'd just smoke so I wouldn't feel that way. I'd only go home to nap, but rarely, because I'd always end up fighting with my mom—she'd yell at me about my grades and about never being home, and I'd just leave. But I didn't think I was addicted—in my mind, I just needed meth to feel okay.

Getting Clean

One morning in July 2003. Connor and I were walking around after a meth binge, and my grandma drove by. We had always been really close—she lived in Spokane—but she hadn't seen me in months, and she freaked: My skin was pale, and I looked completely gaunt because I'd lost a lot of weight. My lips were swollen and purple, and I was just really dirty. "What's wrong with you?" she asked me. "Are you *on* something?" I was so tired, I started swearing at her. I was totally out of control, and my appearance scared her, so she called my mom.

My mom called the cops, and they arrested me as a runaway so they could send me to Daybreak, a 40-day inpatient drug treatment program. I was mad at my grandma, but I wasn't too upset—I mean, I figured I'd just act like I wanted to get clean and then go back to meth when I got out. I didn't get sick from withdrawal, but I still craved it a lot. I calmed myself down by thinking about how I'd get to smoke again as soon as I got out.

Rehab was pretty strict: I'd wake up at 7 A.M. to spend a few hours in class with about 10 other girls around my age, then sit through five hours of counseling. At first, I missed Connor and doing meth a lot. But gradually, I realized that I actually *wanted* to get clean. I started to understand how huge my problem was when the other girls there—users themselves—found out about my meth habit and were like, "Wow, that's *really* bad." And then I got scared: My life had revolved around drugs, and I wasn't sure how to have fun without them. But my counselors kept saying they believed in me, and that helped *me* believe I could stop using. And we'd go on these cool hiking trips and stuff, which made me see that I *could* have fun without drugs. When my treatment was over, I really wanted to stay clean, but I was worried about how I'd do that around Connor. But when I called him to tell him I was coming home, he said, "I want to be single now," I was hurt—but I knew I'd be better off without him.

Facing the World

Last fall, I started my junior year at Summit, a drug recovery high school in Spokane, and it helps a lot to be around other people who are struggling to stay clean. I'm working hard to graduate on time in 2005, and I'm trying to rebuild my relationship with my family. I feel bad about what I put my mom through—I know she worried a lot. But she forgives me, and I feel lucky for that. I still have bouts of wanting to do meth—and in October, I had the chance when I ran into Connor. He asked me to get high, but he looked so horrible—he was really skinny, and his face was all sunken in and broken out in sores—that I thought, I do *not* want to be like that again. And that made it a little bit easier to walk away.

SOCIAL ISSUES
FIRSTHAND

CHAPTER 3

Recovery

A Doctor's Recovery from Drug Addiction

Kimberly Norman Mallin

Despite numerous academic accomplishments and a bright career as a surgeon ahead of her, Kimberly Norman Mallin developed an addiction to the prescription drug Percocet. In the following selection, Dr. Mallin shares the details of her substance abuse, her subsequent treatment, and the rebuilding of her career after losing her job and her medical license. Dr. Mallin is currently a physician in private practice, having completed a family residency program at the University of South Carolina. She and her husband, also a doctor and recovering addict, live on an island off the South Carolina coast.

"**I** sentence you to 12 years in the federal penitentiary."

Those were the last words I ever expected to hear directed at me. After all, I was a fourth-year surgery resident, a wife, a runner, an avid mystery reader. I had graduated magna cum laude from college, finished in the top third of my med school class. So how did I get into this courtroom? Like this:

I started getting headaches during my third year of residency. I tried all of the OTC [over-the-counter: nonprescription] meds, I saw neurologists, I got CT [computerized tomography] scans and MRIs [magnetic resonance imaging], and even tried biofeedback. Nothing worked until the magical day someone said, "Here, take one of my Percocets [a narcotic pain reliever]; they work really well for my headaches." Within 30 minutes of taking the pill, I was sure that I had found the answer to all of my problems. Little did I know, my problems were just beginning.

Kimberly Norman Mallin, "Me? A Substance Abuser," *Medical Economics*, vol. 83, April 7, 2006, pp. 70–74. Reproduced by permission.

Developing an Addiction One Step at a Time

I did know something about addictions. My father had joined AA [Alcoholics Anonymous] when I was in my early 20s. I wanted to know more about his "disease," so I went to a summer conference on alcoholism during my first year of medical school. I had never realized the extent to which Dad's drinking affected our entire family, or that addiction has a genetic component. I also discovered that I had at least one troublesome sign myself—I had experienced alcohol-induced blackouts on a few occasions. Still, knowing that I was genetically predisposed toward alcoholism didn't worry me: I'd just be more careful about my drinking.

As for drugs, I was afraid of them. I'd tried marijuana once and hadn't liked its effects. Besides, I believed those ads that compared "your brain on drugs" to fried eggs. I wanted more than anything to be a doctor, and I knew that I'd need all my brain cells to achieve that goal. After the conference, I went back to med school and started an impaired-students committee. Pretty ironic, in retrospect.

My friend with the Percocet would share only so many. I had *daily* headaches, so what was I to do? I started writing prescriptions—for my husband, some friends, my sister, even my grandmother. Before I knew it, I was filling at least one prescription a week for narcotics. I knew I shouldn't be doing it, but Percocet was the only thing that worked for me. I didn't think about the consequences. I assumed I wouldn't get caught—or if I did, I'd just explain about my headaches.

Getting Caught

About six months after I took the first pill, I was busted. I was in the call room taking a shower when the secretary of the surgery department paged me to let me know some men from the DEA [Drug Enforcement Administration] were there to see me. I was so rattled I took three Percocet tablets before going down to meet them! It turned out that a pharmacist had turned me in for picking up prescriptions in other people's names. (At first, I was furious with that pharmacist; later, I thanked her for saving my life.)

I explained about my headaches and played dumb about the rules. I met with people from the recovering professionals program, signed the contracts they gave me, and agreed to frequent urine tests, convincing them and myself that my problem was inappropriate management of headaches—not addiction. In court, the 50 or so felony charges against me were dropped. I was found guilty of two misdemeanors, and ordered to perform several hours of community service and pay a fine. After the hearing I went out with my sister and had a drink—a strawberry daiquiri with a double shot of tequila—to celebrate not going to jail. After all, I only had a problem with pills, not with alcohol.

The next morning I met with the medical board. I assumed that would go as well as my court date had. Boy, was I wrong. The board members kept asking me about denial, alcoholism, and addiction. I told them I knew all about substance abuse because of my dad. Needless to say, that wasn't the answer they wanted. I was given a temporary license and told if I didn't go to rehab within the next 30 days I'd never practice medicine again. I left for my first treatment center the following day.

The Road to the Bottom—and Back Again

I spent the next three years in and out of treatment centers. I lost my much-prized surgery residency after four and a half years. I lost my medical license—twice. I got divorced. The day I "resigned" from my residency one of the attendings shook his head and said, "You must either want to go to jail, or you're really an addict." I remember puzzling over what must be a repressed desire to experience jail—I couldn't fathom being an addict.

Eventually, I was arrested again and sentenced to the aforementioned 12 years in a federal pen. That sentence was suspended, but the felony charges stuck and I was under house arrest for a year.

I made the newspapers—twice. The first article focused on my fraudulent prescription writing, while describing me as "demure in a peach-and-white striped dress." After the second court case, I was strangely disappointed when there was nothing in the paper for two days. On the morning of the third day, I was having breakfast, casually looking through the paper, feeling safe. A headline caught my eye: "District Attorney Admits to Feeling Sorry for Convicted Felon." I was stunned to find that *I* was that convicted felon!

I wish I could say that after that conviction I got clean and sober and stayed that way. I can't. Recognizing my addiction for what it really was proved extremely difficult for me. Instead, I learned about desperation, failure, inadequacy, and fear. I became a master manipulator and liar—anything to allow me to keep getting my drugs. I persuaded others to give me urine samples, so I always tested negative. I switched from pills to alcohol when I lost my prescription-writing privileges. Although I may have initially started using narcotics to deal with headaches, the drugs had long since become a way of dealing with life. I couldn't imagine my life without them.

The Turning Point

I'm not sure what enabled me to finally overcome the denial and start to recover. The episode that stands out in my mind occurred during the winter of 1995. It was a few days before Christmas, after I lost my license for the second time. I was supposed to go home for the holidays, but couldn't face my family. I called and told them I was drinking again. My parents offered to come get me, but I said No, so they left me alone. (I'll always be grateful to them for allowing me to reach bottom.)

I found myself truly powerless to stop drinking. As if trapped in a continuous loop, I'd drink until I passed out, get up the next morning, go to a 12-step meeting, and stop on the way home to buy more wine. After about five days of this, I woke up to what sounded like a really annoying radio DJ. But when I leaned over to turn off the radio, I realized that it wasn't on. I searched my condo for a radio or TV—anything making noises—and found nothing. I was having auditory hallucinations. My brain was finally failing. Now *that* scared me. I dressed quickly, jumped into the car, and drove to the house of a woman I had met in AA, to ask her for help. That was the beginning of the end.

My sobriety date is April 13, 1996. I had just been kicked out of the third treatment facility I'd been in since asking for help four months earlier. (Once again, I'd been caught drinking while in the treatment center.) I remember standing next to Wayside House in Delray Beach, FL, with nowhere to go. I had no job and no medical license, and I couldn't go home to my parents. I had broken my probation by drinking and leaving the state without permission, so there was the possibility of going to jail if I returned to North Carolina.

Recovery

Something happened that day. I believe it to be a miracle because nothing else had ever deterred me from drinking and drugging my life away. My counselor suggested that I move into the Lighthouse Cottages, a local halfway house. So I put aside my dreams of being a doctor and focused on surviving a day at a time without drugs or alcohol.

For me, graduating from the Lighthouse six months later was as significant as graduating from college or med school. I spent another three years working as a library assistant and staying active in 12-step programs. I came to understand that I was a substance abuser and always would be. The Professionals Resource Network (PRN) in Florida continued to monitor me throughout this time. They helped keep the possibility of a return to medicine alive.

I wouldn't change those years; those hard-earned lessons have proven invaluable for my personal and professional growth. I wouldn't have the strengths I have today if it weren't for those struggles and successes. With the encouragement of the PRN, I decided to try to return to medicine. Not only had I developed a new set of coping mechanisms and a stronger ability to empathize, I understood emotional pain and had learned how to walk through it. I knew what it was like to have a chronic illness. Surely these experiences could only make me a better physician.

Making the Most of a Rebuilt Medical Career

A counselor discouraged me from returning to surgery. Surgery hadn't caused my addiction, but the crazy hours and high adrenaline levels could put me back in a state where I might feel the need for chemical assistance. I still have moments of sadness knowing that I'll never be back in the operating room, humming to the music, tying off sutures, and just feeling the flow of the operation. But it's not worth risking a return to active addiction.

After much thought, I decided to enter family medicine. My physicians' recovery group included several FPs [family physicians] who were successfully juggling busy practices with recovery, and that was what I'd need to do. I applied to 32 residency programs and got a grand total of three interviews. Still, my first interview resulted in a job offer. An intern had unexpectedly quit a New Orleans program and they needed a replacement right away.

I cancelled my other two interviews, quit my library job, put my stuff in a moving van, and headed to Louisiana. I was to meet with the medical board on a Wednesday, prior to starting work the following Monday. I had letters of recommendation from several physicians as well as from the PRN and the residency director I would be working for, all in support of me getting a residency license. At the board meeting I was told, "Take your problem back to your own state. We don't want you here." I returned to Florida, very shaken. But the very next day the Medical University of South Carolina invited me to come for an interview. I was accepted into their family medicine residency program for 1999.

I finished that residency in 2002 and have been in private practice since then, although—appropriately—I've had to jump through a lot of hoops. It took several years to get my narcotic-writing privileges back, and I was only recently released from urine monitoring. Sometimes I can't believe that I'm a partner in a medical practice, that I'm happily married to a special man who's also a physician in recovery, and that we own a home on a beautiful barrier island off the South Carolina coast. I still vividly remember being three or four days sober, sitting in my bathtub at the Lighthouse, sobbing and wondering how I was going to make it another day without drinking.

And yet, I did. Today, 10 years later, I continue to rely on my past experiences to keep me sober and to help others— including my patients, fellow 12-step group members, and other physicians struggling with addictions. I'm not anonymous about my role as a recovering alcoholic physician. I believe that it's important for those of us recovering from this disease to be available to help others who are suffering and can't see a way out. So, I share my story pretty readily. I continue to be active in 12-step groups as well as in Caduceus, the local physicians' recovery program.

There's a saying in 12-step groups: Your worst defects can become your greatest assets. I certainly believe that to be true.

Recovery Saved My Life

Jon Fukuda

Jon Fukuda is a Japanese American born in Los Angeles in 1962. He tells how he began experimenting with alcohol and marijuana as a teenager in the 1970s, became addicted to cocaine in the 1980s, and decided to get help for his problems in 1988.

I am a 41-year-old Japanese American man, alcohol and drug-free since I was 27. From as far back as I can remember, I had a very happy childhood, together with my older brother and sister, and my parents, too. I was born in Los Angeles. When I was 4, my parents picked up and moved to upstate New York for my dad to work. All through school I had fun, on top of my studies. I was an average student, although looking back, I could have done better.

My First Time

As I said, I had a lot of fun. I was about 14 or 15 years old when I started experimenting with alcohol and weed. My friends and I drank a lot and smoked a lot of weed, hangin' out and partying. I remember going into bars when I was 16. Buying weed and alcohol was not a problem. We used to party almost every day and every night. As far as the notion of Asians generally being less capable of tolerating alcohol (the facial "flush" effect), my cousin used to call me "rock lobster," I turned so red. I got past that, and had no problem tolerating alcohol. I'm sure my parents knew about my drinking, because I used to come home at all hours of the night pretty wasted. I don't think they knew too much about the weed. They used to be very cool about it. The worst it got was when I came home one morning at about 7 A.M. My mother was awake and said, next time you want to come home that late, don't bother coming home. That is all she said, and it was back to normal the next day. My dad never used to say anything about it. My brother and sister didn't say anything to me back then, either.

Getting in Deeper

I didn't start snorting coke until I was 21. We moved back to Los Angeles in 1983, where I took part-time jobs at a drug store and at a market. I started buying coke from the guys I used to work with. I bought it because of the buzz I would get. When I would get high, I just felt a tremendous rush. I used to snort it. I paid for it with whatever earnings I made from the drug store and market, which was most of my money.

I enrolled in the Asian American Drug Abuse Program's outpatient service in '86. I can't remember why—isn't that terrible? I guess it was I was spending too much on drugs and thought I could do much more with my life. I was taking unnecessary risks as well. I was in the experimental/functional addiction phase or beyond, not knowing at that time that drug addiction is a progressive disease. It progressed.

No Going Back

After I left the drug store and market, I got a job at a hotel. One of my co-workers introduced me to crack cocaine. After that, there was no going back. I was hooked. Once you start smoking crack, nothing else matters. Sometimes I smoked with other people, but usually I ended up using by myself. Being alone didn't matter, just so I had my drugs. Using crack cocaine was a lot different than just snorting. The feeling is so much more intense. I did anything to get high. The whole world revolved around me getting my drugs. I cheated, lied, and stole to get my drugs. I hurt the people who I loved the most.

My Turning Point

I was arrested for sales and possession, and spent the night in jail. My auntie put her house up for my bail, and when I got home that night, I remember my mother saying that she was glad that I was okay. She gave me something to eat and I probably slept for a day. After my mom and auntie bailed me out, they and a cousin took me out to eat and I broke down crying. After I ate and got some rest, I hit the streets again. Christmas of 1988, I went on an eight or nine day run, meaning that I stayed out and was smoking crack, basically living out of my car. My dad was the one who found me, somehow finding out where the dope spot was. The guy I was with saw my dad approach the car and was going to try and sell him some dope. I said, no, stop, that's my dad. That was the 26th of December, 1988. I totally missed Christmas with my family that year, how sad. Shortly after that is when I decided to go into residential treatment.

Checking in to Recovery

I looked in the mirror and finally said to myself that I needed to check into the program. Even my mother who I hurt so many times, questioned me, saying, "Can't you quit by yourself?" It was so hard checking in because I would be saying I was a failure, falling way short of everyone's expectations. What would my family think? What would my friends think? What would I think? The shame was overwhelming. I would also be admitting that I had a drug problem. Me, a drug problem? Yes, me. I checked into the Asian American Drug Abuse Program's [AADAP] residential program in January of 1989. It was much harder checking into the residential unit than receiving outpatient services. It seemed so much more serious, which it was. There I was in AADAP's residential program, trying to recover from drugs and to find out what the problem was. The program literally gave me my life back. I was able to identify my issues and work through them in order to reestablish myself back in society. I think the biggest issue I had to work through was being assertive. I learned to assert myself. I had a hard time confronting issues, internal and external. I had a hard time saying no. I ended up digging myself into a hole I could not get out of. The residential program worked for me because I needed treatment 24 hours a day. My life was that messed up.

On Being in Treatment

My first day in the program, it went okay. I was nervous, I was away from my family for the first time. My new family—the counselors and other clients—helped me out. Most did, some did not. No problem, that's what groups are for. That's where I would have to practice asserting myself. The program is very structured, with very little free time. You start your day with a 6:30 A.M. wake up call. Breakfast is at 7 A.M. At 8:30 A.M. you clean and cook for the house. You have a few minutes to interact with your peers, then at 11:30 you have lunch. At noon, you can go upstairs for a few minutes to prepare for the afternoon. Later, you meet to discuss any issues that may have developed in the morning. Residents go to a creative expression workshop to explore their creative sides. After dinner, you can go back up to your room if you want. There's an evening meeting at 7:30 P.M. Evenings usually consist of a group meeting on various topics and issues. At around 9:30 P.M. we have a light clean up and then free time until our 10:30 curfew. Lights out at 11:00 P.M.

The last day in the residential program is actually the start of the 4th phase of the program, when you have found a place of your own, which was new to me, never having lived on my own before. That was scary, also. I had to kind of walk through my fears, as I called it. That was 23 months after Day One in the program. After the 4th phase, which is 3 months long, you graduate.

My Life Today

If it wasn't for the staff and peers or my new extended family, I would not have been able to succeed. My immediate family also played a big part by supporting me from the outside. Without them, it would have been difficult to get through the program. I am grateful to everyone who was with me then. I guess the reason that I started using were probably issues like esteem and lack of direction. AADAP's program saved my life. I decided to become a substance abuse counselor, and worked with clients for 11 years. I am now in the personnel department of AADAP. I am working for the same program that has given me so much. Today I enjoy bowling, playing softball, skiing, being with my family, and constantly applying all that I learned in my recovery. I'm pretty happy about how things are going today. A few of my most recent blessings I can count today are a beautiful baby daughter, a beautiful wife, a great family, and a nice little house. Oh yeah, and a life without drugs.

To Everyone Reading This

Be honest with yourself. If you find your life becoming un-manageable, get help. Don't be ashamed to admit that you may be an addict. That is the first step. Otherwise, you know what they say: Jails, institutions, or death. I believe it.

Antidepressants Help a Narcotics Abuser

Maia Szalavitz

Maia Szalavitz is a senior fellow at Statistical Assessment Service (stats.org), a nonprofit organization that monitors the use and abuse of scientific data in the media. She is the author of Help at Any Cost: How the Troubled-Teen Industry Cons Parents and Hurts Kids *(2006), exposé of the "tough love" approach to dealing with teens and adolescents. Szalavitz, who herself was addicted to heroin and cocaine, maintains the usefulness of such antidepressants as Prozac and Zoloft and refutes arguments that such medications mask pain necessary to building character and staying off drugs.*

The first time I did heroin, it was a *Listening to Prozac* moment. Like the patients that psychiatrist Peter Kramer describes in his 1993 book, I felt the way I wished to be, but better than I'd thought possible.

Moments before, I'd been insanely jealous: I'd found out my boyfriend had been with another woman. I was shouting at him in a grotty [grubby] New York welfare hotel. I was filled with self-hatred. I'd been suspended from college because of my involvement with cocaine. I thought I had ruined my life. I was about as miserable and low as could be. And then I wasn't.

I was sitting in a dingy room with peeling paint and crooked furniture. My boyfriend and the couple who lived there desperately wanted me to shut up: He had large quantities of cocaine, they had large quantities of heroin, and neither wanted to attract attention. I'd always resisted heroin be-

Maia Szalavitz, "In Defense of Happy Pills," *Reason*, vol. 37, October 2005, pp. 48–55. Copyright © 2005 by Reason Foundation, 3415 S. Sepulveda Blvd., Suite 400, Los Angeles, CA 90034, www.reason.com. Reproduced by permission.

cause from what I'd read, I knew I'd love it. But my anger got the better of me, and I impulsively snorted the huge line they offered in the hope of quieting me.

Suddenly every atom of my being felt nurtured; every ounce of my essence felt well and light. My jealousy no longer bothered me. I also felt very nauseated—but didn't mind. Nothing could touch me. If I'd been able to feel even close to this naturally on even a semi-regular basis, I thought, I'd never have gotten into such trouble. For once, I wasn't a raw nerve, vulnerable to every tiny stimulus. For once, all the voices in my head that said I was worthless, that told me I was irreparably selfish and vile, had shut up. For once, I felt everything would be OK.

Thinking Techniques to Defeat Addiction

Needless to say, I soon added heroin to my cocaine habit. Although most people don't respond to opioids with the kind of rapture I felt, for me it was love at first sensation.

During the next three years, I deteriorated rapidly, to the point where I found myself injecting both cocaine and heroin up to 40 times a day, broke, and begging a man I detested for heroin. I knew then that I had to stop. The impulse I had to try to seduce him to get the drug broke through my rationalizations about "not really" being an addict. But when I quit heroin that day at age 23, having asked my parents to take me to a hospital detox program for help, I thought I was doomed for life to my vicious internal milieu.

Fortunately, through 12-step programs, I was able to dramatically reduce the crime rate in my mental neighborhood. Using techniques they share with cognitive therapy, my groups taught me, for example, that when I thought others didn't want me around, that was my own, possibly flawed perception—not necessarily the truth of the situation. By behaving like someone I would want as a friend and cutting off the internal debate over whether or not this was "authentic," I was able to gradually stop torturing myself. By doing estimable actions, I gained self-esteem. This made escape with drugs much less attractive.

But these cognitive techniques did not eliminate my bouts of depression, during which all that self-hatred would return furious as ever—and during which I was unable to feel any joy or relief. Twelve-steppers insisted that pain, as the founder of Alcoholics Anonymous put it, was "the touchstone of all spiritual progress," that my depression was telling me something I needed to hear. . . .

Like Myself Again

I began taking antidepressants seven years after I kicked my heroin and cocaine addictions. Both my self-help groups and my individual therapist had discouraged medication, and I'd followed their advice. Twelve-steppers had warned me that avoiding my pain with drugs—any drugs—would only lead back to compulsive behavior.

But in 1996, when I sank into a depression so profound that I was unable to feel the tiniest spark of pleasure, I began to question this position. A publisher had rejected the manuscript for my first book after paying me an advance, and I became so depressed that nothing felt right.

Having decided that the unstructured life of a freelancer was bad for my mental health in such circumstances, I got myself a good job, as an associate producer on a Barbara Walters AIDS [acquired immunodeficiency syndrome, caused by HIV] special. I thought achieving simple goals like getting to the office would make me, at the very least, less anxious, and working to fight AIDS had energized me in the past.

Reaching the Limits of Cognitive Therapy

Before the book was killed, even when I'd felt low, I could usually improve my mood by easing up on myself or seeking social support. I could use my cognitive techniques to recognize when I was grandiosely "catastrophizing"—for example, seeing one obstacle as a sign that everything else in my life was going to collapse. But the new job and the cognitive techniques failed me now. Even love from friends and family didn't help. I knew I'd lose all motivation, even to get out of bed, if meaningful work and socializing didn't at least reduce my dread.

Talking to people or thinking differently couldn't restore my ability to feel good. Even the best of news or most tender expressions of affection didn't interrupt for long the dull terror I felt. When I couldn't stop crying at the office, I finally went to a psychiatrist, who prescribed medication.

The first day I took Zoloft, I was reminded of my earliest recreational drug experiences. Before I'd tried hard drugs, I'd taken many psychedelics, and what I felt after popping that first pill was similar to a feeling I well remembered from using LSD [lysergic acid diethylamide]: a sense in the pit of my stomach that things were about to get strange. Soon, in fact, I was having mild hallucinations: complicated, brightly colored geometric patterns when I opened or closed my eyes. I called my psychiatrist, who told me to halve the dose but recommended sticking with the drug, saying the images would pass.

Transformed by Antidepressants

Two days later, the psychedelic patterns were indeed gone, but the depression and pleasurelessness were as strong as ever, and I found myself missing the hallucinations. At that point, I understood for the first time part of why I'd continued using cocaine long after it had ceased to be at all enjoyable. The distraction of experiencing something, anything, was better than consistent anhedonia [inability to experience pleasure].

Ten days in, I felt the first therapeutic effects. I noticed that I wanted to write and that I felt better after writing. That tiny reward gave me more optimism.

When the medication fully kicked in, I again felt transformed, as I had in that welfare hotel a decade before. Unlike heroin, Zoloft did not make me euphoric, but it provided a similar sense of comfort and safety. I felt like "myself again," as one of Peter Kramer's patients puts it in *Listening to Prozac*. With antidepressants, I wasn't "better than well"; I was the way I am when I'm OK.

Which Is More Real?

In other words, I stopped fearing encounters with friends and dreading the phone. I took pleasure in simple accomplishments. If something awful happened, I felt appropriately upset; the difference was that now I no longer cried uncontrollably while watching families reconnect in AT&T [telephone company] commercials. I began to discover that I wasn't wildly jealous when my (new) boyfriend spoke to another woman—or at least I now had the self-control not to act on those thoughts. I felt competent and far less needy. The reassurance I'd sought from 12-step meetings and phone calls for support didn't seem necessary any more. I could hate myself less because my selfish needs and intrusive worries were genuinely less pressing.

Paradoxically, what the drug gave me was greater control over my own thoughts and behavior and more self-sufficiency. I could still choose to act impulsively when irritated, but I could more easily choose not to. And unlike heroin, the Zoloft did not cause the craving that had ultimately led to obsessive, life-disrupting addiction.

Which was more "real"—my new equilibrium or my previous imbalance? It didn't matter, I decided, because on medication I was better not only to myself but to others as well. I became less needy, less self-centered, less demanding. I will never be a mellow person, but I was certainly calmer. The only downside was greater impatience with people who refused to get help for depression, who still exhibited the flaws I'd hated in myself.

Suicidal Strategy?

During my transformation, I began to recognize that, although the drug companies clearly have an agenda in pushing their view of psychiatric medication, psychotherapists do too. If pills really could overcome depression and addiction without endless digging and talking, they'd be out of business. Just as the "brain chemical imbalance" that supposedly causes depression is part of the pharmaceutical companies' sales pitch, as exemplified by those Zoloft commercials in which a blob with a face turns his frown upside down, the idea that talk is better and deeper and more humanistic is part of the therapists' sales pitch (no matter how much they sincerely believe it).

Each perspective, taken in isolation, relies on an outdated, dualistic view of the mind and brain. The drug companies portray depression as a biological defect that leaves people vulnerable to getting stuck in sadness; the therapists say our thinking and emotional histories trap us there. But neither view precludes the other; both can be right simultaneously because all experience must ultimately be coded by processes in the brain. Given this reality, if the easier, faster way is just as effective, why not use it?

Studies repeatedly find that on their own, drugs and certain talk therapies are about equally effective, with a combination of the two often superior. But the talk therapies which have been proven to work are hard to find. As Vanderbilt University psychologist Steven Hollon puts it, "The treatments shown in clinical trials to be specifically effective for depression are still not widely available."

Antidepressant opponents such as Peter Breggin argue that drugs can have terrible side effects, so even unproven talk therapies are preferable. Recently, for example, evidence about the relationship between suicide and selective serotonin reuptake inhibitors (SSRIs) such as Prozac and Zoloft has begun to emerge. Not only can they increase suicidal behavior among depressed people, but a study published in 2000 in *Primary*

Care Psychiatry found that some normal people given these medications become suicidal. In clinical trials, suicide rates are two and a half times higher in subjects given SSRIs than in those given placebos, according to David Healy, a psychiatrist at Cardiff University. He estimates that up to 5 percent of the population may have severe negative reactions to SSRIs that can, in the worst cases, lead to suicide.

Side Effects vs. Benefits of Drugs

But that doesn't mean the drugs don't help others. For the majority of patients, SSRIs seem to reduce suicidal thoughts and suicide itself. Suicide rates in the U.S. have declined since the introduction of these drugs. Given that at least 50 million Americans have taken SSRIs since Prozac was approved in 1987, if their main effect was to increase suicide, the opposite should be true. Further, several studies that have compared local SSRI prescribing rates with corresponding suicide rates have found that the medications are linked with fewer, not more, self-inflicted deaths.

Other SSRI critics—such as Harvard psychiatrist Joseph Glenmullen, author of the 2001 book *Prozac Backlash*—note that SSRIs don't seem to have much advantage over placebos in clinical trials. This argument, like the suicide warnings, overlooks the importance of individual variations. Nearly every psychiatrist who has used SSRIs has stories similar to mine and those in *Listening to Prozac*. When you match the right person to the right medication, the positive change is remarkable and unmistakable. David Healy's research has shown that certain personality traits are associated with extremely positive (and others with extremely negative) reactions to these drugs.

The fact that good matches occur only in a small subset for each drug—and that bad matches occur as well—means that clinical trials wash out the contrast between the drug and placebo groups. Most people have a small positive effect, some are transformed, and some are made worse; grouping them together obscures these differences. Which is why Healy, the author of the 2004 book *Let Them Eat Prozac: The Unhealthy Relationship between the Pharmaceutical Industry and Depression*, still prescribes SSRIs and does not want them banned.

Side Effects of Talk Therapy

When it comes to side effects, it's also important to recognize that drugs are not the only treatments that can cause harm. Some forms of psychotherapy can be at least as damaging.

It is now clear, for example, that hundreds if not thousand of families were split, many irrevocably, by false memories of incest created in "recovered memory" therapy. Some people received lengthy prison terms as a result of false accusations; many simply lost the invaluable emotional and health benefit of having a close, loving family. Others (including children) were hospitalized for years, tied to beds, and told they had to release "alter" personalities implanted during Satanic rituals in order to be healed. This sort of thing happened in mainstream hospitals such as Chicago's Rush Presbyterian as recently as the early '90s. "The entire history of the recovered memory phenomenon, each and every example, is an example of harmful therapy," says Richard Ofshe, a University of California at Berkeley sociologist and co-author of the 1999 book *Therapy's Delutions: The Myth of the Unconscious and the Exploitation of Today's Walking Worried*.

Other talk side effects come from therapies that rely on cult-like tactics or become actual cults. Synanon, the Northern California–based drug rehab organization, forced men to get vasectomies and pregnant women to have abortions if they wanted to remain part of the group—and told them they would return to their addictions and die in the streets if they left. Members were made to split up with their spouses or partners and rematched with others by the cult's leader.

To this day, the largest addiction treatment providers in the U.S., Daytop and Phoenix House, base their care on the confrontational "attack therapy" of the Synanon system, and program graduates trained in Synanon's methods staff and run many programs. Although some programs have tried to eliminate the excesses of this approach, reports of humiliating treatment are still common despite research showing it is harmful.

Both Synanon and the Los Angeles–based Center for Feeling Therapy often beat patients; the New York–based Sullivanian therapy cult resulted in numerous bitter child custody cases. And then there is "rebirthing" therapy, which in 2000 killed a 10-year-old girl in Denver. The "therapy" was an attempt to improve her difficult relationship with her adoptive mother by smothering her while trying to replicate the conditions of birth.

Destructive Talk

It's not just wacky therapies that can harm. According to research by Yale psychologist Susan Nolen-Hoeksema, depression can be exacerbated by focusing obsessively on "the causes and consequences" of personal problems. Therapies that encourage people to ruminate on the origins of their depression thus can make the condition worse. According to a 1999 study published in the *Journal of Personality and Social Psychology*, many commonly used anger management treatments, which urge clients to "get it out" by yelling and hitting inanimate objects, actually increase rage.

Then there is the matter of all the time and money spent on therapy that could be used for more productive pursuits. Ofshe, who distinguishes between life problems that can be helped by counseling and support and major mental illnesses such as schizophrenia and clinical depression, tells me "all the evidence for years and years has shown that people who practice using psychodynamic techniques, all the therapies derived from [Sigmund] Freud, every time anyone tried to treat any real mental disorder, it was a waste of time and money and when real treatment [was developed], they were diverted from something that could be helpful."

Many see such side effects as less problematic than those resulting from drugs, because the patient has a choice whether to follow the therapist's guidance, whereas drug side effects are involuntary. Yet talk therapies cannot work as their proponents intend if the patient doesn't comply, and noncompliance in addition treatment can result in incarceration, so in that sense the side effects derive just as directly from the treatment.

As Healy points out, talk therapy can "wreck families, can wreck lives just as much as pills can. People tend to see the risks from pills. They think if they [do] talk therapy, there can't be any risk. But no one ever got raped by a Prozac pill."

Although there is no way of knowing how many rapes are committed by mental health professionals, a survey of 1,320 psychologists by researcher Kenneth Pope, published in the journal *Psychotherapy* in 1991, found that at least half of therapists reported treating one or more patients who'd had a sexual relationship with a prior therapist. The respondents believed more than 90 percent of the patients had been harmed by the relationships. Earlier surveys found that between 7 percent and 12 percent of male therapists (including psychiatrists, social workers, and psychologists) admitted to engaging in a sexual relationship with a client at least once.

Amotivational Syndrome

Even if drugs outperformed both placebos and talk and had no side effects, there would still remain the complaint that these medications kill pain rather than address its cause. In a 2001 letter to the *Archives of General Psychiatry* for instance, a psychiatrist described an alcoholic who kept drinking because Prozac made him feel better, leaving him less determined to get sober. The letter also mentioned a woman who lost her resolve to leave an abusive boyfriend after taking Paxil [an SSRI] for several weeks.

But while the data from clinical trials of SSRIs in treating addictions are mixed, the findings are either positive effects in reducing alcohol and other drug use or no effect, not reduced recovery. And while some people may remain in abusive relationships because antidepressants dull their desire to get out, others find the courage to leave after being treated with SSRs. Without better research focused on this issue, it's impossible to know which reaction is more common.

My own experience suggests that whether a drug paralyzes or activates you has as much to do with where you start emotionally as with the drug itself. Some heroin addicts find that the drug (or a maintenance substitute such as methadone) allows them to be kinder and more open to others because it reduces their overwhelming feeling of vulnerability and oversensitivity; others find it makes them stone cold and numb. It depends on where they begin: If they are too self-conscious and anxious to socialize, lowering the volume of those sensations can help; if they are already indifferent, the drug will make that worse.

Antidepressants are similar. Although they don't offer the unearned euphoria that so disturbs anti-drug crusaders, they do, like heroin, strengthen the voice that says it's going to be OK which is so important for getting through tough times and which some people may not be able to access without chemical help.

Does It Really Build Character?

It's the same with physical pain: Too much agony can be as life-destroying and consciousness-contracting as too much anesthesia, and the determination of how much is too much depends both on the original level of pain and on how the drug changes it. Just consider whether you are more agreeable to and nurturant of your loved ones when you have a ferocious toothache, or when the pain has been properly medicated. One cannot discuss a good or a bad drug—only a good or bad drug for a specific person and purpose.

The notion that emotional pain and difficulties inevitably lead to growth and maturity is a largely unexamined assumption with deeps roots in Western religion. Almost everyone can name individuals who believe their painful challenges made them into better people. This is part of why "tough love" approaches to emotional problems continue to thrive and why "easier, softer" approaches such as medication are so often dismissed. As Fox News Channel commentator Sean Hannity put it in 2002, "I've had a criticism of [psychiatrists] for a long time. I think they're too quick to overprescribe drugs and offer chemical solutions. They totally discount the spiritual side of the human nature."

But such critics rarely consider how often pain truly leads to growth—and how often it leads to stagnation, self-destructive escape attempts, and greater emotional damage. Few question whether the anecdote of the survivor made stronger is more common than that of the victim devastated. Most people can easily cite examples of both. Since pain is so common, however, we want to think it's essential to growth. We want it to *mean something*—and don't like to imagine we could learn to be happier, better people without it.

Being Jim Carrey

Focusing on the value of pain misses the critical role of pleasure in learning. Probably the most difficult task facing human babies is learning to speak, yet it occurs almost completely without punishment. Babies learn to talk because babbling feels good and earns them smiles and praise, and because speaking lets them get what they want far more efficiently and comfortably than they do by crying. They don't learn language by being hurt when they get a word or phrase wrong or hit for not talking; they grow into speaking by basking in love.

"In most cases," says Bruce Perry, a child psychiatrist and expert on childhood trauma, "the acquisition of any new piece of information is much more related to repetition than to anything else, and the most powerful biological source that fuels repetition is pleasure." People learn most lessons better when the experience engages and excites them, not when it's dull or painful. While overcoming challenges is part of the process, if there is no sense of reward and competence early on, most people are far more likely to quit than persevere. In fact, according to Perry, threatening and potentially painful situations make people behave less intelligently because their actions are guided by the lower, more reactive parts of the brain.

For the mental health professions, these findings mean the ability to feel joy—or at minimum, to feel OK—is at least as important to recovery from depression and anxiety as discovering the origin of the pain. In fact, in many cases restoring the ability to feel pleasure may be all that is needed. The source of the trouble could be some misfiring neurons, stuck in the angst of 20 years ago or simply signaling for no emotional reason at all. Regardless of the origin of the problem, if you fix the neurons, the distress is gone. A number of studies indicate that effective depression treatments, whether talk or drugs, lead to regrowth of neurons in an area of the hippocampus that is often damaged by emotional trauma.

While this phenomenon might be unsettling if, as in the movie *Eternal Sunshine of the Spotless Mind* drugs made these changes by erasing the memories that make us who we are, there's no evidence that antidepressants do that. And those who argue that we should be able to impulsively act out our prickly, irritable, depressive characteristics to provide human variety are not usually the ones who have to live with those who do so.

Fear of Dependency

One final argument for preferring talk to drugs is fear of dependence. Some antidepressant drugs do produce painful withdrawal symptoms, and it is unconscionable that some patients are given these medications without appropriate warnings and without first having tried other, less problematic treatments. But there's also no doubt that some talk therapies create dependence every bit as worrisome. Therapy cults aside, just think of those analysands who have therapy four hours a week and never make a decision without first consulting their shrinks.

While it's always better to have fewer needs, physical dependence on medication, in and of itself, needn't be a problem if the drug is readily available and safe. If the drug improves one's ability to work and love, who is being hurt? We're all dependent on air, food, and water, and maintenance medications will become a fact of life for most of us as we outlive the ages which our bodies evolved to reach. Whether the medication treats high blood pressure, pain, or depression shouldn't matter.

Suffering Is not All It's Cracked Up to Be

This is not to say we have anything close to perfect medications—and for many people, the tradeoff between side effects, risks, and benefits weighs against taking those currently available. In this connection, full disclosure of the data on current drugs and more research and openness on those in development is critical.

Nor do I believe there is never lingering emotional distress that needs to be understood and conquered, or that there is no role for talk therapy or self-help. Many studies, including a 2002 review in the *American Journal of Psychiatry* and a more recent head-to-head trial published this year [2005] in the same journal, have found that certain talk therapies are just as effective as drugs. A 2003 study published in the *Proceedings of the National Academy of Sciences* even found that for people with childhood trauma, one such therapy was more effective.

But evidence-based therapy is hard to find outside university research studies. The therapy that helped the childhood trauma victims more than drugs, for example, was a cognitive-behavioral treatment that focused on dealing with current problems, not searching for their roots in the past. It wasn't the kind of "depth" treatment talk therapy proponents usually advocate.

No More Superiority

Few patients outside of studies get therapy based on what the research finds effective; most practitioners ignore the data and do what their "clinical experience" suggests. Recognizing this gap, government agencies such as the Substance Abuse and Mental Health Services Administration have distributed literature and sponsored initiatives aimed at bringing "research into practice." But while the situation is far better than it was 10 or even five years ago, both researchers and patients say there's a long way to go. For talk therapy to be a genuine alternative or supplement to medication, the methods covered by insurers should be proven safe and effective, just as the Food and Drug Administration requires for drugs. Mental health advocates have long called for "parity" between coverage of mental and physical illnesses, but it makes no sense to cover talk unless therapists practice proven treatments.

In addition to insisting on evidence of effectiveness, mental health professionals need to understand that suffering isn't necessarily good for the soul. My own experience has shown me that therapy, self-help, and medication all have value. It has also shown me the pitfalls of each. Both depression and addiction have biological, sociological, and psychological dimensions that vary in importance depending upon the individual and his or her situation. This complexity means that no one solution will work in all cases and that the right approach for any given person may change over time.

I can say this: Painful talk therapy isn't morally superior to medication or to therapy that doesn't go "deep." Pleasure can be just as important for emotional recovery and growth as pain, if not more so. That's why drugs sometimes are the better fix.

CHAPTER 4

Parental Views
on Drug Abuse

Talking to Kids about Drugs

Jeanette Kennett

Dr. Jeanette Kennett is a senior lecturer in the School of Philosophy and Bioethics at Monash University in Australia and the mother of four children. She is the author of Agency and Responsibility: A Common-Sense Moral Psychology *(2001), a study of "common sense" versus philosophical understandings of human behavior. In the following essay, Kennett argues that government antidrug propaganda suggests that parents take a counterproductive approach to discussing drugs with teens.*

Once upon a time I was almost as conservative and hardline about the evils of drug use as [Australian Prime Minister] John Howard and his chief adviser on drug strategy, Brian Watters, could have wanted. But that was once upon a time when my children were still young and I still read to them and watched them play basketball and netball on Saturdays and football on cold muddy Sundays, and drove them to their pottery classes and music lessons. Zero tolerance made sense in our small world, a world where I controlled the borders, a world where I knew what was best for them. But our world grew larger and so did the children. Our experiences together have shaped my views as much as I have shaped theirs. That is how it should be, though it was not easy to let it be.

I thought back to those early times as I watched the federal-government-sponsored series of advertisements depicting families and young lives destroyed by drug use—heroin use, of course, though that is not an especially popular drug. I found the advertisements unexpectedly affecting. In many ways they rang true. They showed that these things—drug related arguments, crimes, death, grief, turmoil and bewilder-

Jeanette Kennett, "Talking to Your Kids," *Meanjin*, vol. 61, June 2002, pp. 34–41. Reproduced by permission of the author.

ment—do happen. Even in nice middle-class homes like mine and yours, to well-loved, ordinary, happy kids with seemingly bright, open futures.

What did not ring true in this campaign was the analysis of and the solution to the problem presented. The implied analysis, given the innocent beginnings of these stories, is that it is drug use *simpliciter* [simply of itself] that is to blame for the depicted slide into degradation: teenagers thieving, prostituting themselves, behaving violently, ending up on the streets, in the lock-up, in the morgue. By this interpretation, drug use is not just potentially damaging to one's health, it is *corrupting*; that is what justifies and indeed morally requires that we get 'tough on drugs'. That is why drug use is properly a criminal offence.

A War on Children

This message is made even clearer in the government pamphlet that accompanied the television campaign. In highlighting the scheme that allows drug users to be diverted into compulsory assessment it says: 'if users want to be free of the criminal justice system they have a personal responsibility to work to be free of drugs.' The scheme is not available to 'persistent offenders' (that is, those whose problems are more serious and intractable). *They* will be dealt with in the criminal justice system. Drug use is so seriously immoral that those who persist in such immorality deserve severe sanctions.

This view pervades the government approach to both recreational and problematic drug use—indeed it makes no distinction between the two. Having confronted both, my hard-won view is that drug use is not criminal because it is corrupting—it is corrupting, where it is, very largely because it is criminal. A war on drugs turns out to be, as [film actor] Michael Douglas's character in *Traffic* observed, a war on our children. And we are expected to take up arms.

The solution offered in this television campaign and more generally by the government to the problems presented by drug use is to block that use. The government for its part, as we know, is trying to prevent drug use through law enforcement. It is proudly 'tough on drugs'. The government booklet reinforces the message that we parents need to be tough on drugs too. We have to make it clear to our children that we won't tolerate their using drugs and we have to make it clear that the rules apply not just at home but wherever they are. We must not assume that they know this, and we must not assume that our children are not at risk. As the advertisements show, kids from good homes use drugs too. But the clear message is that good parents can block the risk by talking about the dangers of drug use, pointing out its criminal nature, and setting firm rules. If we give our children the information they require, they will be less likely to rely on misinformation from friends or from those who seek to recruit them into drug use. 'Who is talking to your kids about drugs?' the ads intone. It had better be us.

Antidrug Propaganda Creates Distrust

It seems to me that there is a serious internal tension in this campaign to get parents to talk openly about drugs with their teenage children in a climate of criminal prohibition and moral panic. Moreover, the government is confused about the proper processes, aims and outcomes of genuine open discussion with one's children. A so-called conversation in which parents seek to impress on their children the dangers of drug taking, in a single-minded effort to dissuade or protect them from experimentation, is likely to be short and unproductive. Parents, according to my sixteen-year-old daughter, are the last people you would talk to about drugs: they don't know what they're talking about, and if you did approach the subject with them they would *start* to worry that you were taking drugs and increase their surveillance of you. If they found out you *had* taken drugs they would 'go ballistic'. The information in the drug booklet that is supposed to be a resource for parents in these conversations is hopelessly one-sided and it therefore lacks credibility in our children's eyes.

Certainly, a quick read of the list of 'symptoms' of use of the different drugs makes it utterly mysterious why anyone would ever be tempted to take them. The booklet for the most part carefully skirts the reason why most ordinary kids try drugs, namely that it's reputed to be fun and that it often *is* fun. So on the one hand, as my daughter pointed out, you have the booklet with its unrelenting focus on the bad effects of drugs plus a bit of jargon designed to obscure description of the pleasurable effects; on the other you have your friends, who are having 'mad fun' and appear to be unscathed by their experiences. Who are you going to believe about what certain drugs do?

The reluctance of many teenagers to talk to their parents about drug use is a bad thing. It's especially bad because if they do have an adverse reaction to something they try, their parents are likely to be the last people to know, and their children and those they are with may be too afraid to seek help at all. Anna Wood, the Sydney teenager who died at the age of fifteen after taking ecstasy, was plainly very ill for around five hours before her parents and an ambulance were called. 'We weren't scared for ourselves,' one of her friends said, 'we were very scared for Anna. We knew that if Anna's mum found out what she'd been doing she would never let us see Anna again.'

Teach Kids Risk Management

I do not know if the outcome would have been any different for Anna and her family if she and her friends had not been afraid to seek help earlier. I do know that I don't want my daughter, my sons and their friends to be too scared to contact me. But to get that kind of trust I need to have a real conversation with them. Like all conversations, one about drugs may stray down unexpected paths. After all, it is not and should not be just *my* conversation—it is not a meeting that I run to a strict agenda with predetermined, government-approved outcomes for the items listed for 'discussion'. None of my conversations with my children go like that; they are quick to spot an agenda, and when I try to predetermine the outcomes a conversation turns very quickly into a face-off. We are talking about what it is like to talk to real teenagers. They don't come out of wholesome *Father Knows Best* sitcoms, they have minds and agendas of their own, and adolescent propensities for storming off, slamming doors, sullenness, scorn and rebellion are only aggravated by *Father Knows Best* attitudes.

A real conversation about drugs must move beyond prohibition, beyond scare-mongering, beyond laying down 'clear boundaries', beyond implacable opposition to what very large numbers of teenagers are doing, opposition or no. Otherwise, sullenness, resistance and deception are what we will get and what we will deserve. We need to listen as well as talk, for we have things to learn too. And what I have learned over eight long years of issuing diktats [harsh decrees or orders], of failed attempts to secure the borders, of remonstrating, arguing, talking and listening, is that my opinions and concerns, though noted, and mostly understood and respected, are not the final arbiter of their actions. And so I've come to the conclusion that I must talk to my children not just about the dangers of drug use but also about safer drug use, about what they can do to minimise the risks of experimentation and about getting help quickly if things go wrong. But of course government policy doesn't envisage us having *that* kind of conversation, because the very purpose of the conversations is supposed to be to drug-proof our children—to *prevent* experimentation. Tell them how dangerous it is, and the thought is they won't do it.

This is pie in the sky. Since when were teenagers deterred from trying something pleasurable because they were told it was also risky? Of course some teenagers are risk-averse, as I was, and will stay away from drugs, as I did, but very many are not, and neither more information nor a cosy chat with mum and dad will change that. I have had it pointed out to me calmly and reasonably, by the most rational of my sons, that a great many activities, including many undertaken purely for pleasure, such as skydiving or skateboarding, involve risk. Drug use for recreational and spiritual purposes has been a feature of probably every human society. This does not constitute any kind of positive argument for drug use, but the onus is surely on me to show why it is intrinsically worse than other inherently risky but legally permitted activities. I may not think the pleasures of drug use, or the insights it might sometimes permit, are worth the risk, but there comes a time when they will decide, not me, which risks they take. This transition takes place during the teenage years, it often happens sooner than we parents would like, and we know that some of our children will make bad decisions and some of them will be hurt. But what is the alternative? Risk is part of life and we don't want them to be ruled by fear. We need to teach our children to manage risk, to reduce it, not just avoid it. We don't stop them from skateboarding, we urge them to wear safety gear. We don't stop them from going into the surf, we tell them to swim between the flags. If we can't stop them from using drugs we should at least ensure that they have the relevant safety information.

Crying Wolf

Genuinely open communication with your kids is a good thing and leads to a better relationship. But it doesn't, in my experience, mean they won't experiment with drugs. It means that you're more likely to hear about it if they do. Moral hysteria about drugs surely produces the same secrecy, the same shutting out of parents from their children's lives as moral hysteria about sex did in my growing-up years. They do it to protect us as well as themselves. In the case of drugs they do it also because we make ourselves irrelevant. The dangers we are trying to alert them to are unlikely to be taken seriously when the booklet that outlines them is so undiscriminating. The government strategy encourages parents to cry wolf.

Are we really meant to be *equally* opposed to sniffing inhalants, heroin use, the occasional joint and the use of ecstasy? Once again the government pamphlet suggests we should be. 'All illicit drugs carry risks and are dangerous. There is no safe level of use', it proclaims. This is a significant exaggeration. Though I am very concerned about the use of marijuana by teenagers I can't manage to convince myself, and I'm sure I couldn't convince them, that smoking *small* quantities of marijuana, two or three times a year, say, is particularly dangerous, more dangerous than riding their bike to school each day. And though many teenagers have been deterred from ecstasy use by the tale of Anna Wood, many others tell you, correctly, that such deaths are extraordinarily rare—far more rare than deaths from overdose of that gentle-to-the-stomach household staple, paracetamol [acetaminophen; a pain reliever, such as Tylenol]. If we won't distinguish between more and less dangerous substances and practices, between occasional and heavy use, between having fun and covering up life's problems, how can we expect our more knowledgeable, independently minded teenagers to pay any attention to what we say?

Honest communication that acknowledges both the ill consequences and the pleasures of drug use, as well as the possibility of experimentation, gives parents credibility in the conversation and opens the door to discussions of how to reduce the risks of such experimentation. We can do this while making it perfectly clear that we'd rather they didn't use drugs at all. But, of course, those of us who do this are guilty of 'sending the wrong message' and allegedly condoning what is still criminal activity. The government policy is such that parents can't comply with it. You either take the prohibitionist line or you have a real conversation. You can't do both.

Are Drugs Inherently Bad?

So much for what parents can do to prevent or limit drug use. Where we lose the battle, can the law win the war? The evidence suggests not. Recreational drug use among teenagers and young adults is extraordinarily widespread. It is normal. The law doesn't deter. And it doesn't help families after the fact, in cases where drug use becomes problematic. Shaking the law in front of your addicted child does no good. They can't just stop. And how many parents will call in the police anyway? Criminal sanctions deter openness about drug use, not use itself. They overlay an already painful situation with fear and shame.

But not only is the policy of prohibition ineffective in achieving its stated aims. It is actively immoral. To see this, let's consider the bogeyman drug, heroin. What is it that parents fear when they think about heroin addiction? It seems pretty obvious. Addiction has serious ill consequences: the risk of overdose, contamination, blood-borne diseases, poverty, malnutrition, homelessness, exclusion and marginalisation, prostitution and criminal activity, police, courts, prison, rape, suicide. Of course we fear it. This is not the kind of life anyone would want for their child. But now let us ask if these bad consequences follow from the drug use itself. Are they inevitable?

Suppose you tell me that a medical program is available for my addicted child. Among the benefits listed are these: the treatment stops people 'hanging out'; it stabilises them so they can lead a normal life, including returning to school and work; it brings about a dramatic reduction in the frequency of theft and other drug-related crime. On the health front it reduces the risk of blood-borne infection, it removes the risk of contamination and it helps those treated lead a healthier life, including improved diet and sleep. As a parent I'd be delighted with such substantial benefits. Would my relief and joy be ruined when you also told me that my child would still be addicted to opiates? For the treatment I am talking about is methadone and methadone *is* an opiate. The Victorian [Victoria is a state in Australia] Department of Human Services information booklet for users makes it clear that you are still addicted to opiates while on methadone. Indeed, the information pamphlets warn those on the program that methadone withdrawals are particularly severe (which is why some addicts reject it). How then can this opiate save the lives that its evil cousin heroin destroys? It must surely be different in some significant way.

Prohibition, not Drugs, Causes Evils

It is. It is legally available to addicts on prescription and that means that it is clean, cheap and safe in the right dose. Addicts can stop worrying where their next dose is coming from and get on with their lives. As they could if their preferred opiate, heroin, was available on prescription also. Now if that is the only significant difference between the two, and no-one claims that there is any other difference, our policy-makers are engaged in a serious and culpable piece of doublethink. We were supposed to be worried about the bad and corrupting consequences of heroin use; those consequences are what justify its prohibition. A moment's rational thought, however, reveals that there is no internal connection between the two. All the evil consequences are the consequences not of heroin dependence but of the externally imposed conditions in which the use takes place, in this case conditions of prohibition, rather than regulation.

It is public policy that ensures that addicts cannot get a pharmaceutically clean, secure and affordable supply of heroin. It is public policy, not heroin dependence, therefore, that pushes them into crime, poverty and homelessness, and even death. These are evils that we as a society visit upon users for no better reason than that we disapprove of their drug use. This is true moral evil and policy-makers are knowingly or recklessly implicated in it. If opiates were intrinsically corrupting and damaging to one's health the methadone program could not have the benefits claimed for it. But it does have these benefits. I have seen them for myself. It is just that it is not for everyone. Some people would do better on, and be more willing to enter, a heroin program.

Poor Character Is Not Illegal—Why Drugs?

The Australian Drug Foundation's booklet states: 'As with all opiates, methadone alone in its pure form will not cause any damage to the major organs of the body. Prolonged use will not cause any physical damage apart from *tooth decay* (my emphasis). Have we been fighting the war on heroin only to protect our children from tooth decay? Is there anything else that could possibly justify this piece of public policy?

You might argue that drug addiction *is* intrinsically bad, not necessarily for bodies but for souls. It undermines the person's autonomy and reveals a certain weakness of character. I'm not so sure of the character implications but I am prepared to agree that I'd much rather my children didn't become heroin addicts even under more benign social conditions. I'd also much rather they didn't become diabetic or paraplegic or develop a heart condition or Parkinson's disease. These conditions, too, would restrict their autonomy in certain ways. And on the character front I'd rather they didn't tell lies, cheat on their partners and show a callous disregard for the suffering of refugees. But note that none of *these* things are illegal. We don't arrest our politicians. It's not illegal in most circumstances even to fail to render assistance to someone who is injured or dying. But it is illegal to put a needle in your own arm if it contains heroin and not insulin.

I am writing this on Palm Sunday [the Sunday before Easter]. I attended the rally for refugees. So did one of my sons.

We listened to speeches urging a repeal of the Border Protection Act [an Australian law intended to keep refugees out of the country] and a recognition of our common humanity. Later he met up with his brother for their weekly basketball game. It was a late evening game so I weakened and picked them up afterwards. The days of driving them around are not quite over. Another son spent the day rehearsing a show for Melbourne's Comedy Festival. His last show was *Catch 22*, about the absurdity of another war. My daughter had lunch with her boyfriend, who is a refugee from East Timor. They caught a tram home afterwards and he stayed with her till I got back from basketball. Tomorrow they will go to school, work and university, they will keep appointments, they will see friends, they will make plans. I'm proud of them all.

Among all the comings and goings of this day one of the family made a trip to the chemist. 'What does the methadone do for you?' I asked one day. 'It keeps me warm,' was the reply. This daily journey, part of a much longer one towards inner peace and warmth, need make no difference to anyone else's day. What difference would it have made if heroin rather than methadone could have been provided there?

Selected Sources

National Drugs Campaign Information for Families, Public Health Division, Commonwealth Department of Health and Ageing (December 2001), http://www.health.gov.au/pubhlth/nide/families.html.

Methadone Treatment in Victoria, User Information Booklet, Public Health Division, Victorian Government Department of Human Services (March 2001), http://www.dhs.vic.gov.au/phd/0009093.

Australian Drug Foundation booklet, http://www.adf.org.au/drughit/facts/methadone.html. Mike Gibson, 'The Ecstasy and the Agony', *Daily Telegraph*, Sydney, 24 May 1996.

A Mother's Loss Fuels Her Antidrug Message

Ginger Katz

Ginger Katz, a mother of two who lost her oldest child when he overdosed on heroin in 1996, founded the Courage to Speak Foundation to help fight drug abuse in high schools. She was named Woman of the Year in Connecticut by the Connecticut Post *in 2002. Katz describes the death of her son Ian and how she turned her heartbreak into positive action to help teens stay off of drugs.*

My son, Ian, died in his sleep of a drug overdose on September 10, 1996, the day before he was going to enter a rehabilitation program. I found him at 6:00 A.M. just before I was going to meet a friend for our morning run. We rushed Ian to the hospital in the hope that he could be revived, but he had died a few hours before. I never thought that I would ever have to bury my 20-year-old son. My heart was broken.

At first, I did not want anyone to know how Ian died. When my brother asked me what killed Ian, I went catatonic and just stared at him wide-eyed. I had witnessed Ian's relapse the day before he died. I knew what the toxicology report would tell us, but I could not bring myself to say it. Nor was I able to tell my daughter Candi, who has Down Syndrome, that her brother had died. Her father had to give her the devastating news.

I could not sleep the night before Ian's burial because I was thinking about what I would say to the hundreds of people who would be at the service. I woke my husband and told him that I could not go to the funeral, that there was no

Ginger Katz, "The Courage to Speak," *Principal Leadership, High School edition*, vol. 3, February 2003, pp. 33–36. Copyright © 2003 National Association of Secondary School Principals. Reproduced by permission.

way I could get through it. Knowing the truth and not wanting to reveal it was holding me back. Before that night ended, an idea, perhaps more of a revelation really than an idea, came to me. My husband and I decided that we would share what we had suffered to prevent other people from suffering. We would tell them the truth about how Ian died.

They say the truth will set you free and I believe it. Once I made the decision to be honest and tell others about Ian's drug abuse, I was able to sleep. The next day, I was the strong one at the funeral. I held the many young girls, pretty in their long black dresses, in my arms as they cried uncontrollably. And I comforted the boys, who to me now looked more like men than boys although they sobbed like little children. Their grief left me even more determined to devote myself to halting the creeping evil of drugs. But before I could teach others, I had much to learn. I applied for and received scholarship money to attend courses on addiction and recovery, and I researched drug abuse on the Internet. Once I felt ready, I had to decide where to begin.

A Principal Becomes an Ally

Armed with my new wealth of substance abuse information, I approached Dewey Amos, the principal of Norwalk (CT) High School. When Dewey came to Norwalk in the late 1980s, he was the housemaster in charge of Ian's house. Later, he became the school's principal. He knew Ian well and was rocked by his death. The two of us talked about Ian's high school years—his friends; his sports; and his mercurial relationship with his first love, their public displays of affection and sometimes anger, and how Dewey had called them into his office more than once to tell them to behave. As we reminisced, we both cried. He had not lost one of his students to drugs up to that point, and Ian's death had a profound effect upon him.

Our meeting was cathartic, but more than that, it was motivating. By the end, Dewey promised to devise a plan for halting drug abuse in his school, and I agreed to develop a program to relate Ian's story to students. We both knew that what we were proposing to do would take courage because the silence that surrounds the disease of addiction is deafening. To succeed, we would have to find a way to inspire others to break through the patterns of denial and squarely face the risks and consequences of drug abuse.

Taking Action

True to his word, Dewey began working with his staff to develop a plan to fight drug use at Norwalk. He knew that if he was going to change behavior, he would first have to change attitudes. There are many reasons why schools—private as well as public—cover up their drug problems and claim not to have them when, in fact, nearly all schools do. People move into a community based partly on the reputation of its schools and drugs scare them away. Teachers and staff members with career ambitions want to be associated with a winning school, not one tarred by rumors of drug abuse or police arrests. Worst of all, hostile parents often storm the principal's office complaining and refusing to believe the truth about their children.

In spite of the resistance he knew he would face, Dewey devised a bold zero-tolerance drug prevention plan that includes many elements:

Consequences. Any student caught with drugs will be suspended for 10 days and not allowed back in school until that student's parents agree that upon readmission the school may drug test their child at its discretion.

Security. A beefed-up security team of six will be stationed in the halls to monitor student activity during school hours and after-school activities.

Parents. Parents who protest the school's disciplinary measures against their child will be invited to a conference with their child and all others involved in the incident that required the discipline. The meeting will go on until the truth comes out, and once it does, parents, school officials, and the student will agree to a course of action.

Police. The school will maintain a relationship with local police to identify students who are serious violators (e.g., gang members, drug dealers, and gamblers), and appropriate measures will be taken to rehabilitate these students or isolate them if they are repeatedly breaking the law. (Parents' fear of arrest is understandable, but few realize that student offenders are usually required to do community service and that once that requirement is satisfied, the stain is removed from their record. Kids get a second chance.)

Counseling. The school will expand its partnership with local adolescent counseling services to provide professional help (both in-house and off campus) for troubled teens. Counselors, who often don't see drug abuse in their clients because they are concentrating on other dysfunctions, will be encouraged to consider the possibility of drug use as a catalyst to the behavior that got the teens into trouble.

Positive alternatives. The school will create clubs and programs to offer positive alternative activities for students, such as an Entrepreneur's Club, which takes students to markets to buy goods at wholesale prices and bring them back to the school to sell at retail; links to programs run for youths by local clergy; and a school Jobs Program that allows kids to make honest money.

Zero Tolerance

It took time, but Dewey's plan became fully implemented and widely praised. It has reduced drug use among Norwalk's students by their measure and has eliminated dealing in the school. Today, the school's teachers and staff members who were reluctant to go along with the plan are glad to be associated with a school that backs up its zero-tolerance policy with action, and they take pride in being part of a school that has successfully stood up to its drug problem. Norwalk students who feel pressured to try drugs use the school's swift and sure action policy as an excuse not to. It gives them a badly needed refusal tool.

The last facet of Dewey's plan called for speakers to be brought into the school on a regular basis. Some carry messages to students to inspire them to lock onto a plan for their future. Others, like me, talk directly about drugs and behavioral problems related to drug use. This drug prevention-speaking plan began with my presentation in early 1997, when I took my first stab at telling Ian's story.

The Courage to Speak Foundation Is Born

Dewey assembled 150 kids to hear my debut. I told this first audience of Ian's academic and sports successes, and I showed them pictures of my handsome son smiling his blinding smile from grade school to the last days of his life. I spoke openly and plainly about the down days, describing bizarre events like the night a boy set Ian's car on fire in front of our house and burned down a tree on the lawn. I thought it was an accident until the next day when we found beer bottles next to the car with gasoline in them—crude Molotov cocktails—and realized that it was arson. I later learned that violence such as this goes hand in hand with drug use because of money owed, drugs undelivered, or just plain drug-induced hostility. At the time, Ian's car fire made no sense to me because at that point I had no knowledge of his drug use. A fight he picked at school concerned me, but I chalked it up to youthful indiscretion.

What was ultimately Ian's fatal addiction, I explained, began in eighth grade with a puff of tobacco, a sip of beer, and a bit of weed. As he progressed through high school, Ian's grades were respectable, and he played dazzling lacrosse his junior and senior years. Ian won the lacrosse "Attackman" award during his last season with 26 goals and 17 assists.

Because of his success in sports and academics and his popularity throughout high school, I did not realize that he was using and dealing, except for one incident that made me vigilant. When Ian was in 10th grade, he and some friends were picked up by the police, who found marijuana in the car. Ian denied smoking it, but I decided to have him drug tested just the same. I insisted that he be tested twice, the second time without warning because I had a gut feeling that he had switched his first urine sample. I was right. The test results declared the first sample negative and the second positive for marijuana.

Optimism Grows

Parents, I told my audience, have good instincts and they must learn to trust them. I discovered after Ian died that the negative sample belonged to a girlfriend's baby brother because, the girl told me, "None of the kids were clean." After that incident, Ian continually tested clean. I believed that Ian was back on track and I had high hopes for my son, especially when he went off to college.

I stopped worrying about drugs until Ian's dad called to say Ian was snorting heroin in college. My breath was taken away. My life changed. When Ian first came home from college, I was ashamed. I spoke to him about his drug abuse and vigilantly looked for clues that he might be using. But the better I got at sniffing out clues, the better he got at hiding any evidence, wearing sunglasses to hide his eyes; stashing pot in his stereo speakers; and changing his clothes before he came home so I would not smell tobacco, alcohol, or pot.

With some difficulty, we convinced Ian to enter a day treatment program in June of the summer he died and, once again, the problem appeared to be fading. Ian's last summer was the best summer of all. From June through September, he played tennis with me, golf with his father, and worked reliably and responsibly for the town park system. But more than that, our charming, athletic son was back smiling his blinding smile. That happy summer filled me with optimism.

Crushed Hopes

But drug addiction has a way of recurring. On September 9th, Ian spent the afternoon with the kids he had shared drugs with at college and, in their company, he relapsed. That evening, I discovered that he had snorted heroin. When I asked him about it, he cursed and threatened to storm out of the house. I stopped him at the door and said softly, "If you want my help, just ask me." He did ask for help and agreed to call his doctor to be admitted to a rehabilitation program the next day. Because he made this choice willingly, I was soothed and hopeful, but the sad truth is that it was too late. Ian had ingested too much heroin on September 9th, so his resolve to get help had not come in time to save him. He died in his sleep that night.

I wrapped up my first presentation with advice that I have continued to give to children for six years. I urge each and every one of them to find adults in their lives who will listen to their issues and concerns and their frustrations and fears. Find a trusted relative, a favorite teacher, a coach, or a clergy member and talk out your problems. Hold nothing in, I tell them. When kids are downhearted, angry, or confused, they often make bad choices and turn to alcohol, drugs, and sexual promiscuity that lead to depression, feelings of isolation, and increased anger. Ian had bottled things up, and it had killed him.

When I finished speaking, teachers and staff members, as well as students came forward to tell me their personal stories and reveal problems in their inner circles. One student sent me an e-mall message that read, "I don't want to use drugs because I wouldn't want to hurt my mother." Others confessed problems to me and asked me to help them find adults to confide in. An adult wrote to me, saying, "Expecting another drug abuse prevention presentation, we were completely unprepared for how powerful this. . .would be." If I had any doubts about speaking out, the reaction of my first audience dispelled them. With my presentation, I hoped to encourage others to summon the courage to speak out about the substance abuse problems affecting their lives and look for solutions to them. Hence the name of my foundation: The Courage to Speak.

The Signs of Abuse

I speak to students and adults, and in the adult program, I point out that if I did not fully appreciate the seriousness of Ian's habit, I was not the only one. His pediatrician, his teachers and counselors, even some of his friends failed to notice his drug abuse. In fact, the psychiatrist who counseled him during his last summer wrote in his notes, "Ian is not at risk."

What 20-year-old who has been snorting heroin for four months is not at risk? It is human nature for people to deny the unthinkable. We have been raised to think that drug addicts are down-and-out people living on the streets, not winning kids on track for success. Yet it is just those kids who, seduced by drugs, become tomorrow's homeless or addicted adults. If we are going to save our students from drugs, we must recognize and acknowledge the unmistakable signs of drug abuse early and take action, as Dewey Amos does, as soon as the signs of drug use are sighted.

Some signs of substance abuse are:

- A sudden drop in grades or change in social performance
- Withdrawal, isolation, depression, or fatigue
- Truancy
- Excessive influence by peers or change of friends
- Hostility and lack of cooperation

- Deteriorating relationships
- Loss of interest in hobbies or sports
- Changes in sleeping and eating habits
- Evidence of drugs or paraphernalia
- Physical changes, such as red eyes, runny nose, frequent sore throats, rapid weight loss, or bruises from falls.

A Tough Program

Each year, 15,000 children die from abusing drugs and many more fall short of their potential because of addiction, but they can be saved if their abuse is nipped in the bud. When teachers and school staff members see students exhibiting behavior that conforms to the signs of drug use, they should take swift action for those caught with drugs, get parents involved, and followup with drug testing and rehabilitation. Parents need to be convinced that there is something far worse than their child getting caught using drugs: their child *not* getting caught doing drugs. By the time Ian's use was uncovered, he was already in the grip of addiction.

Using discipline and a guiding hand as his tools, Dewey has markedly reduced his schools drug problem. With candor and honesty as my tools, I have changed the way tens of thousands of people approach drug abuse. We both have been honored for our work by schools, service organizations, and government for which we are grateful. But the greatest rewards seem to come when we least expect them.

A father whose family was falling apart because of his daughter's drug abuse called me to say "My daughter is alive, safe, and drug-free and our marriage is on solid ground because we listened to the Courage to Speak presentation and got help." At the 2002 Norwalk High School graduation ceremony, a girl who had been caught with Ecstasy, suspended, reinstated, and drug tested, thanked Dewey as she picked up her diploma. "You saved me," she said, "and I will never forget you."

A Father's Shocking Discovery

Thom Forbes

Thomas Forbes, a reporter and recovering alcoholic, writes about searching for his heroin-addicted daughter Carrick in New York City's Lower East Side, while reflecting that he has little or no control over his 17-year-old daughter's life.

I'd slept fitfully for an hour or two at most. At 6 A.M., I shook my wife, Deirdre.

"We've got to get rolling," I said.

Carrick Doesn't Come Home

Deirdre asked what I intended to do. I said that I was going to New York City to look for Carrick, our seventeen-year-old daughter, who had not returned home the night before. About midnight, we had called Carrick's friend Vanessa and learned that they'd gone down to the East Village the previous afternoon, a Sunday, against our wishes. Vanessa had last seen Carrick about 9 P.M. at Grand Central Terminal, when she had boarded a train home to Bronxville. The small village where we'd lived for fourteen years, Hastings-on-Hudson, is on a different line than Bronxville and the train departs twenty minutes later.

"Carrick seemed fine," Vanessa told us. "I thought she was getting the next train home."

Deirdre said that she would call some of Carrick's other friends as I headed downtown. This was not the first time Carrick had disappeared. I tried to sound confident as I told Deirdre that wherever she was, I was sure nothing bad had happened to her. The words just hung in the air as I kissed her and walked out the door.

Thom Forbes, "Our Odyssey: Enter Chaos, Carrick Doesn't Come Home," *The Elephant on Main Street: An Interactive Memoir of Addictions and Recoveries*. Reproduced by permission.

It was Nov. 5, 2001. At 10 A.M., Carrick was due at the headquarters for the Students for a Free Tibet on East Ninth St. between Avenues B and C in Manhattan, where she had been volunteering for the past month. Community service is a part of the curriculum at Walkabout Program, an alternative public high school for seniors who, like Carrick, have had difficulties in traditional settings. Since she was in eighth grade, Carrick had attended several programs for kids who have educational, emotional, psychological, or substance-abuse problems, all of which had afflicted our daughter. . . .

I called Deirdre after I arrived at Grand Central Terminal. She said she had talked to Megan, a girl who was interning with Carrick at Students for a Free Tibet. Carrick had become friendly with someone who called himself Chaos, Megan told Deirdre, and she might be with him. He hung out in Tompkins Square Park. She described him as pierced and heavily tattooed. Megan told Deirdre she would arrive at Students for a Free Tibet's offices a little after 10, and told her she'd meet me there.

"Tell your husband not to look for Carrick himself," she said. "He might scare her away."

Students for a Free Tibet

Students for a Free Tibet headquarters were on the ground floor of a decrepit factory building on the north side of East Ninth St., closer to Avenue C. Inside, it looked like a time warp of '60s activism—cast-off furniture, posters on the wall, beer cans strewn about, squashed chips on the floors, ashtrays overflowing. My first reaction was that it did not seem to be an ideal environment for a seventeen-year-old in recovery. The organization's soft-spoken executive director apologized for the mess when I arrived. He said there had been a staff party for Halloween. I told him why I had come. He had not heard from Carrick, he said.

I sat down on a squishy couch, exhausted, as a couple of other staff members arrived. In a hushed voice, the supervisor filled them in on why I was there. Megan finally came through the door, later than I'd expected her. I introduced myself. She said she thought she knew where Carrick was, but she had to go to get her alone. About forty-five minutes later, she returned. She had not found Carrick, she said, but she told me there was someone who wanted to talk to me. He knew where Carrick was, but he was nervous. Would I meet him?

"Of course," I said. "Is it Chaos?"

"No. His name is Champ," she said.

"She's Hooked"

Holding an unlighted cigarette and looking like a beneficent padrone [master], Champ sat in a booth at the Odessa diner, sipping coffee I later paid for. The word on the street, he said, was that Carrick and Chaos were hiding out in an abandoned theater. He asked me if I knew where that might be because he didn't really know the area. I said no, but it could be the huge abandoned building on the corner of Eighth St. that was covered with signs protesting an impending eviction. He said we'd have to get them out ourselves, and that he needed my word that I would not get the cops involved. I said okay, although I dreaded entering what I envisioned to be a nest of rooms filled with crackheads.

"I gotta tell you something you don't wanna hear," he said.

I looked at him and nodded. Nothing he could say was worse than what I'd imagined.

"She's using heroin, Tommy," he said.

"How much and for how long?" I'm sure my voice that sounded much calmer than I felt. "Is she shooting or snorting?"

"It's bad, Tommy," he said. "She's hooked."

"No Cops"

He didn't know how long she'd been using, though, or whether she was shooting it or not. He told me that getting her back would be complicated by the fact that Chaos, the guy she was with, owed somebody some money for some dope they'd scored that morning. I was suspicious, which must have showed. I asked Champ if he meant that I'd have to pay somebody off, and he said we'd have to wait and see. He suggested we try to get more information from the people in the park. I gave him $60 for his help so far. I wanted him to know that I was prepared to reward him if we found Carrick, and that I'd pay others if I had to. We left the coffee shop.

"Tommy. I want to make sure we're clear on one thing," Champ said as we crossed Avenue A. "No cops."

I took a deep breath.

"I've heard a lot of stories and I think I've got a pretty good sense when somebody's conning me," I replied. "I don't think you are."

I said that partly because I wanted to hear in my own voice whether I believed it or not; I sounded like someone trying to convince himself that he's doing the right thing. It had reached the point where I was just reacting to circumstances. My only goal was to take Carrick home. And I knew that, in reality, I was easily conned. Carrick herself had proven that to me time and again.

Buying Information

Inside the park, Champ approached a group of people sitting on a bench. I kept walking on the path to the left. At best, I looked like a reporter, if not a cop. Champ came over and told me he would have to give them some money. He pulled out the $60 I'd given him. I thought he wanted to pay off the dealer that Chaos had supposedly beat that morning, and told him that I didn't think it was a good idea. Champ said that wasn't the case.

"Nobody gives up anything on the street for nothing," he said. "Listen, they say that Chaos and your daughter are sleeping in the band shell near the bridge. Do you know where that is?"

Offhand, I didn't. He suggested that I walk back to the group with him. He took aside a wiry young man with closely cropped hair, handed him $20, and introduced me as someone who was looking for Chaos because I wanted to buy some crack. Sizing me up through squinting eyes, the guy asked how much I wanted and why I wanted to buy it from Chaos. I told him I didn't want any crack; I was a father looking for his 17-year-old daughter, who was with Chaos.

"That your daughter?" he said, with a slight Spanish accent. "She's a beautiful girl. Shit. I wished someone was looking for me."

He said that Chaos and Carrick and another guy were in the old band shell in the park by the Williamsburg Bridge and told me how to get there. After I thanked him, he asked me if I was sure I didn't want some of his crack.

"Chaos isn't a good source, man. Not for crack. Dope, yes. Not crack."

I shook my head.

A Walk in the Park

Champ and I walked through the park and across Ninth St. toward the river. I told him that I wanted to stop at Students for a Free Tibet to let them know what was going on. He was leery. He told me that he'd level with me. He had an outstanding violation for jumping a turnstile and that if the cops got involved, they'd take him in. As suspicious as I was that Champ had done more than beat the subway fare, I assured him again that I was not calling the cops. I did call Deirdre, though. I wanted her to know where we were heading. I wasn't sure it was the right decision, I said, but I saw no alternative.

Champ and I discussed a lot of things as we headed toward the river. He did most of the talking. He told me that he had been in the army. He said he'd come from a large family, and his father would beat the shit off out the boys when they did something wrong. His twin sister was a junkie who was always stealing from him until she had overdosed and died. He thought we should drop a nuclear bomb on Afghanistan to wipe out Al Qaeda. What did I think?

We crossed the footbridge over the FDR [named for Franklin Delano Roosevelt, U.S. president from 1933 to 1945] Drive and walked south along the park path. Few people were out. It was a blustery day, the wind swooping in from the river. The longer we walked, the more I began to question what we were doing. I had played softball in the park ten years before, but my memory of a band shell was vague. I checked a pocket street atlas I'd brought from home, but it only showed swings, baseball diamonds and a tennis court. I told Champ that I hoped we weren't being set up. He resented this. I assured him that I wasn't suggesting the *he* was setting *me* up. Of course, I wasn't sure of that either. . . .

A Bad Rap

I asked him about his jail time [Champ had been in prison]. It was a bad rap, he said. He'd been minding his own business when he saw a guy beating up a woman outside a bar in New Jersey. He told the guy to stop. They got into a fight. He punched the guy in the ribs. The ribs cracked and punctured his lung and he died. Because he had been a boxer, Champ's hands were considered a lethal weapon, and he had been convicted of manslaughter. Then he almost got killed in jail when a black guy stabbed him in the neck with a shiv—he stopped to show me the wound—while he was playing poker. The motivation had something to do with cigarettes. He also told me that his partner had shot him several times. He wanted to show me these wounds, too, but I was beginning to feel numb to his tales of woe and just kept walking.

We passed two Latino youths who looked to be about twenty. One was pushing a stroller. I assumed a baby was in it but didn't look. As soon as they went by, Champ asked me if I had another $20. He wanted to ask them if they'd seen Chaos and Carrick. I pulled a bill out of my pocket. He called after them. At first, they were suspicious. Then Champ told them that I was the father of a seventeen-year-old girl who had run away from home and that I just wanted to get her back. This seemed to click with the one not pushing the stroller, a tall young man with smooth skin and a sweet face. He said that two guys and a girl who fit my description were sleeping in the back of the band shell. He'd seen Carrick around, he said. He had no idea how young she was, and said he understood why I was doing what I was. He said his name was Danny. He offered to come with us. We tried to figure out what to do about the $20. The guy with the stroller wanted a cut of it even though he wasn't accompanying us, but Danny didn't seem to trust him to split the money later. I was reluctant to pull my wallet out of a concealed pocket of my jacket, but I did. I gave the guy with the stroller $10, and Champ told Danny he'd get the other $10 after we were sure that Carrick really was where he said she was. That seemed to be okay with him.

We got to a wire fence on the north side of the band shell, which was in terrible shape. Champ suggested that he and Danny look inside the structure, and that I wait by the fence alone. They were afraid Carrick would take off if she saw me coming. They went through a rip on the river side of the fence, and stopped at the wall of the structure for a few seconds. As they walked back, I could not discern from their expressions what they'd seen.

Going in Alone

"She's there," Champ said, his voice trailing off, as if there was a hitch. My heart raced—part joy, part anxiety. Then, like a soldier who'd been behind the enemy lines, Champ described the scene. He said the three of them were asleep under some blankets on a raised platform.

"It's not stable, Tommy," he said. "It could collapse at any time."

Champ then turned to Danny and told him he could go, handing him a $10 bill from the money I'd given him earlier.

Danny shook his head.

"I want to make sure this man gets his daughter back," he said.

Champ started to get agitated. He asked me what I wanted to do. I didn't really trust anybody at this point. But I figured having two people around was better than one, so I said Danny should stay.

"I think it's better if I go in alone, though," I said. "I'm going to make it clear to everybody that I don't want any trouble. I just want Carrick to come home with me."

I felt like I was in an outtake from the movie *Traffic*, which I'd seen recently. The protagonist, played by Michael Douglas, discovers his addicted teenage daughter turning tricks in a squalid hotel room to support her habit. I hoped that it would not come to a fight, as it had with Douglas's character, or that I'd face a weapon. But I also felt a foolish confidence, as if the righteousness of my mission would protect me.

"I Don't Want Any Trouble"

I slipped through the fence. Champ and Danny remained at the opening, presumably ready to back me up. I walked quickly across the vaulted chamber, which was filled with debris and trash. A makeshift ladder leaned against what looked like a sleeping loft about eight feet off the ground in the southwest corner. I climbed it. Carrick was in the middle of two lumps under blankets, cuddled against a figure in the far corner. I leaned across a completely submerged body and shook her. I wondered what to say. Should I be firm, or conciliatory?

Should I ask, or demand?

"I'm here to take you home, Carrick," I said. "I don't want any trouble."

It took a couple of shakes before Carrick opened her eyes and looked at me.

"I don't want any trouble," I repeated.

She said nothing; closed her eyes. The young man in the foreground sat up and stretched, but seemed oblivious to me.

"C'mon, Carrick," I said.

"Give me a couple of minutes," she muttered, as if I was rousting her for school. Her face was dirty; her hair matted. She looked stoned. She shook the body in the corner, and started to whisper in his ear. I heard her say, "baby." He lifted his head, which was swathed in a bandana. I saw a crescent tattoo on his temple. He glanced at me through dazed eyes, and looked away.

I climbed down from the ladder to allow them to, I hoped, say goodbye to each other. I walked to the middle of the bandshell so I ostensibly was out of earshot but could still see them. I worried they would take the opportunity to hatch some escape plan. Carrick lay down. I gave her a minute or so.

"C'mon, Carrick," I said, "time to go," again assuring everyone that I wanted no trouble.

She sat up, slowly gathered some loose gear, stuffed it into her leather backpack and pecked on the cheek the man who I assumed was Chaos. She said goodbye to the other figure, who was heavily pierced, and crawled over him. She would not take the hand I offered to assist her as she came down the ladder. At the bottom, I hugged her. She responded hollowly. She did not seem to be there. She greeted Champ warmly, though, and they immediately started talking. . . .

Danny Believes in God

Danny and I talked. He asked me if I believed in God. I said not in the sense that most people do, but that I respected many religions and thought that anything that helped people was good. I was spiritual, I said, but not religious. He said he couldn't imagine that there was not a God. He said he was in recovery himself, from drinking and drugging. He was going to meetings again after having slacked off. The streets were tough, he said. A popular kid in the neighborhood had died a few weeks before when he shot up some dope laced with rat poison. Everyone knew the pusher responsible, but he'd disappeared.

"When we find him," Danny said, "he's dead."

Danny told me that he'd seen Carrick snorting heroin in East River Park the night before with the girl she was with, whom he had not seen before. I was surprised—not by the fact that she had taken heroin, which I'd already become resigned to, but because it was evident that, like a small village, everybody seemed to know what was happening to everybody else in Losaida, as the neighborhood is known.

Danny said he'd had a tough life himself, but he wasn't complaining. His father had owned several nightclubs and was prosperous, but he got into drugs and lost everything. Danny used to fish with his father, he said, and they loved each other, but he died several years before. His mother drank, he said, and beat him. She had thrown him out of her apartment in the Jacob Riis public housing project, but he was on his way to see if she'd take him back because he couldn't stay with his girlfriend any longer. We shook hands at the corner of Ave. D and East Tenth St. I gave Danny a twenty and wished him luck. He said that if I ever wanted to know more about the neighborhood, just ask for Danny. Everybody knew where to find him.

"I'm Gonna Pay You Back"

After Danny left, I watched Champ and Carrick prattle like drinking buddies. I wasn't entirely sure that they weren't in cahoots. Maybe Carrick had convinced Champ I was an evil dad and she'd tear down the street while he restrained me. I broke into their conversation, telling Champ that I'd seen a jogger that morning throwing jabs and repeating loudly, "keep dancing, keep dancing." He agreed that boxing was all about where you put your feet, and started to give us a demonstration on the sidewalk. A woman with a stroller nervously swerved around us.

Carrick said she was hungry and suggested that we eat at an Indian restaurant. I asked Champ if that was okay with him, and he said that he'd never had Indian food. I saw a couple of other ethnic restaurants on the street; Champ said he was basically a meat and potatoes guy. We wound up at a Polish restaurant, where he ordered a hamburger. I devoured my kielbasa; Carrick didn't finish her meal. Neither, to my surprise, did Champ. Junkies don't seem to have much appetite, I learned later, except for crap like sugary cereal and ice cream.

Back on the sidewalk, Champ asked for directions to Tompkins Square Park, which was only a couple of blocks away. It struck me that, despite his swagger, he was a rube who had not ventured far from familiar quarters. He took me aside, whispering conspiratorially.

"Listen, would it be okay if I called Carrick to see how she's doing?" he asked. "Maybe I could even come and visit her sometime. She says she'd like to take some more boxing lessons."

"Sure," I said. "Why don't you keep the calling card."

"Really? Hey, thanks, man. I could use it to find a job."

I looked into his eyes and gripped his hand as firmly as I could.

"I want to thank you for saving Carrick's life," I said. I did not think I was exaggerating, I slipped him another $20.

"I really mean that," I said.

"It was nothing, man, nothing. Soon as I get on my feet, I'm gonna pay you back."

Carrick and I headed to the station for the No. 5 train. When it came, she took a seat, and I stood over her. Her eyes closed and her head slumped. . . .

Two Questions

As soon as we boarded the Metro North train to return to Hastings-on-Hudson, Carrick slouched in the seat and shut her eyes. I told her she had to answer two questions before I'd let her sleep.

"I want honest answers because we can't help you to help yourself otherwise," I said.

"How long have you been using heroin? And are you shooting it as well as snorting?" "I've never touched that shit," she said. "Whoever told you otherwise doesn't know what the fuck they're talking about."

I knew she was lying, but what could we do except wait for the results of a drug test? And then what? We'd have her tested for the HIV [Human immunodeficiency virus, which causes AIDS] virus, too, for sure. And hepatitis. But what beyond that? Should we force her to go to another rehab? Using what reward as bait? What punishment as a threat?

I felt I'd accomplished nothing. On the surface, I had dragged my daughter out of the belly of the beast. But deep down I knew it was illusory. When I saw her lying between two scuzzy junkies in that crumbling band shell, I knew how low she was prepared to sink to in order to use drugs. Like a pipe to the head, it struck me that Deirdre and I had little, if any, control over our 17-year-old daughter's fate.

Organizations to Contact

The editors have compiled the following list of organizations concerned with the issues debated in this book. The descriptions are derived from materials provided by the organizations. All have publications or information available for interested readers. The list was compiled on the date of publication of the present volume; the information provided here may change. Be aware that many organizations take several weeks or longer to respond to inquiries, so allow as much time as possible.

Alateen/Al-Anon
1600 Corporate Landing Pkwy
Virginia Beach, VA   23454-5617
(888) 4AL-ANON • Fax: (757) 563-1655
Web site: www.al-anon.alateen.org/

Alateen is a part of Al-Anon, an organization based on Alcoholics Anonymous's 12-step program, but directed toward people whose family members are struggling with alcoholism. Alateen is specifically for teenagers whose families are affected by alcoholism. The Web site offers information about finding local meetings and ordering Alateen literature about coping with a family member's substance abuse problem.

Alcoholics Anonymous
PO Box 459, New York, NY   10163
(212) 870-3400
Web site: www.alcoholics-anonymous.org/

Look under "Alcoholics Anonymous" in any U.S. or Canadian telephone book to find local groups immediately.

Alcoholics Anonymous (AA) is a fellowship of men and women who work together to stay sober and help others to recover from alcoholism. The organization was founded in the 1940s by Bill Wilson, the originator of the 12-step program for attaining sobriety. The Web site presents information on the organization and how to find local AA meetings.

Alternet

77 Federal St., San Francisco, CA   94107

(415) 284-1420 • Fax: (415) 284-1414

Web site: www.alternet.org/drugreporter

Alternet is an online news magazine and Internet community devoted to fair, even-handed reporting on important issues. The Drug Reporter section of Alternet's Web site contains articles relating to drugs and the drug war that take into account differing viewpoints from those most commonly seen in the mass media.

Cool Spot

Web site: www.thecoolspot.gov

A Web site produced by the U.S. government's National Institute on Alcohol Abuse and Alcoholism, the Cool Spot offers literature directed at teens about alcohol, peer pressure, and finding help for alcohol addiction. The National Institute on Alcohol Abuse is a part of the U.S.-government organization the National Institutes of Health, which studies various topics in health and medicine.

Drugscope

40 Bermondsey St., London   SE1 3UD
  U.K.

(020) 7940-7500 • Fax: (020) 7403-6169

E-mail: info@drugscope.org.uk

Web site: www.drugscope.org.uk/druginfo/drugsearch/home2.asp

Drugscope is an independent British organization that provides information to policy makers and the general public in order to understand drugs and reduce the risks of drug taking. Their Web site presents detailed information on drug production, use, addiction, laws, and the properties of various drugs ranging from caffeine and tobacco to heroin, marijuana, and other substances such as khat and mandrake.

Erowid
PO Box 1116, Grass Valley, CA   95945
Web site: www.erowid.org

A member-supported organization that runs an online clear-inghouse of information about psychoactive substances and issues related to them. The site offers a plethora of information on drugs and their effects, laws, scientific studies, users' experiences, the use of drugs in many cultures, and non-drug approaches to spiritual awakening.

Health Canada
Office of Demand Reduction, Ottawa   ON K1A 0K9
  Canada
(613) 941-3974 • Fax: (613) 957-1565
E-mail: bedrugwise-droguesoisfute@hc-sc.gc.ca
Web site: www.drugwise-druguesoisfute.hc-sc.gc.ca/

Health Canada is the Canadian government's agency for the study and improvement of health, health treatment, and health policy. Its "Be Drug Wise" Web site provides information for youth about drugs, drug abuse, and getting help.

Narcotics Anonymous
PO Box 9999, Van Nuys, CA   91409
(818) 773-9999
Web site: www.na.org

Narcotics Anonymous (NA) is an organization similar to Alcoholics Anonymous (AA) in its structure and aims. NA grew out of AA in the 1950s. A fellowship of people who work together in local groups to overcome drug addiction and stay clean, NA bases its program on a version of the 12-step approach to sobriety from alcohol. The Web site offers online versions of NA literature, self-help texts, and a search engine for finding local chapters.

National Association for Children of Alcoholics
11426 Rockville Pike, Suite 301, Rockville, MD   20852

(888) 554-COAS • Fax: (301) 468-0987

E-mail: nacoa@nacoa.org

Web site: www.nacoa.org/kidspage.htm

The National Association for Children of Alcoholics (NACoA) is dedicated to improving the lives of individuals whose parents are alcoholics. NACoA's "Just for Kids" Web site contains resources for kids to learn about alcohol, alcoholism, coping with a family member's alcohol problem, and finding organizations and information to help.

National Clearinghouse for Alcohol and Drug Information

PO Box 2345, Rockville, MD   20847

(800) 729-6686

Web site: http://ncadi.samhsa.gov

The National Clearinghouse for Alcohol and Drug Information is a U.S.-government organization sponsored by the U.S. Department of Health and Human Services. Their Web site promotes government publications on drug and alcohol abuse and treatment.

National Council on Alcoholism and Drug Dependence

22 Cortlandt St. Suite 801, New York, NY   10007

(212) 269-7797 • Fax: (212) 269-7510

E-mail: national@ncadd.org

Web site: www.ncadd.org

The National Council on Alcoholism and Drug Dependence (NCADD) is devoted to fighting the stigma and the disease of substance abuse. The organization offers educational materials, information, and confidential help. Its National Hope Line provides referrals to treatment programs, and its National Intervention Network line provides education and assistance to families and friends of drug and alcohol users. The Web site contains fact sheets and information about substance abuse, some of which is directed at youth.

National Institute on Drug Abuse
6001 Executive Blvd. Room 5213
Bethesda, MD   20892-9561
(301) 443-1124
E-mail: information@nida.nih.gov
Web site: www.teens.drugabuse.gov

The National Institute on Drug Abuse (NIDA) is a part of the U.S-government agency the National Institutes of Health, which sponsors studies pertaining to various health-related topics. The NIDA specializes in scientific study and information dissemination regarding drug abuse. The Web site "NIDA for Teens" provides teenagers with a variety of information about drugs.

Students for Sensible Drug Policy
1623 Connecticut Ave. NW, Suite 300
Washington, DC   20009
(202) 293-4414 • Fax: (202) 293-8344
E-mail: ssdp@ssdp.org
Web site: www.ssdp.org

Students for Sensible Drug Policy is a youth organization devoted to examining and reforming drug policy in the United States. Its Web site details various issues concerning drugs and the drug war.

Youthline
13 Maidstone St., Auckland, Ponsonby
  New Zealand
(09) 376-6645 • Fax: (09) 376-6650
E-mail: urge@xtra.co.nz
Web site: www.urge.co.nz

Youthline is a New Zealand-based organization that offers support services and information to youth on a variety of issues, including drugs and drug abuse. Their Web site "Urge" gives detailed information about common drugs.

YouthNet UK
2–3 Upper St., 3rd Floor, London   N1 0PQ
  U.K.
(020) 7226-8008 • Fax: (020) 7226-8118
Web site: www.thesite.org.uk

YouthNet is a U.K.-based charity that provides information about issues of interest to youth, including sex, relationships, drinking, drugs, work, study, housing, law, and finances. Their Web site includes extensive information on drugs.

For Further Research

Books

Caroline Jean Acker, *Creating the American Junkie: Addiction Research in the Classic Era of Narcotic Control*, Baltimore, MD: Johns Hopkins University Press, 2002.

David Boyum and Peter Reuter, *An Analytic Assessment of U.S. Drug Policy*, Washington, DC: AEI Press, 2005.

Jefferson M. Fish, ed., *Drugs and Society: U.S. Public Policy*, Lanham, MD: Rowman & Littlefield Publishers, 2006.

Hamid Ghodse, ed., *Addiction at Work: Tackling Drug Use and Misuse in the Workplace*, Burlington, VT: Gower, 2005.

Meyer D. Glantz and Christine R. Hartel, eds., *Drug Abuse: Origins and Interventions*, Washington, DC: American Psychological Association, 1999.

Meyer D. Glantz and Roy Pickens, eds., *Vulnerability to Drug Abuse*, Washington, DC: American Psychological Association, 1992.

Avram Goldstein, *Addiction: From Biology to Drug Policy*, 2nd ed., New York: Oxford University Press, 2001.

James E. Hawdon, *Drug and Alcohol Consumption as Functions of Social Structures: A Cross-Cultural Sociology*, Lewiston, NY: Edwin Mellen Press, 2005.

Richard Isralowitz, Mohammed Afifi, and Richard Rawson, eds., *Drug Problems: Cross-Cultural Policy and Program Development*, Westport, CT: Auburn House, 2002.

Yifrah Kaminer, *Adolescent Substance Abuse: A Comprehensive Guide to Theory and Practice*, New York: Plenum, 1994.

David Patrick Keys and John F. Galliher, *Confronting the Drug Control Establishment: Alfred Lindesmith as a Public Intellectual*, Albany: State University of New York Press, 2000.

Sana Loue, *Diversity Issues in Substance Abuse Treatment and Research*, New York: Kluwer Academic/Plenum Publishers, 2003.

Judith Rumgay, *The Addicted Offender: Developments in British Policy and Practice*, New York: Palgrave, 2000.

Bill Sanders, ed., *Drugs, Clubs, and Young People: Sociological and Public Health Perspectives*, Burlington, VT: Ashgate, 2006.

Thomas Stephen Szasz, *Ceremonial Chemistry: The Ritual Persecution of Drugs, Addicts, and Pushers*, Syracuse, NY: Syracuse University Press, 2003.

Sarah W. Tracy and Caroline Jean Acker, eds., *Altering American Consciousness: The History of Alcohol and Drug Use in the United States, 1800–2000*, Amherst: University of Massachusetts Press, 2004.

Periodicals

Cate Bailey, "Pain Meets Poison: The True Story of How One Teen Huffed Her Way to Rock Bottom and Almost Died," *Junior Scholastic*, March 14, 2003.

Jason Bane, "The Scariest Drug Epidemic You've Never Heard Of," *Teen People*, December 2003.

Community Care, "My Kids Use Heroin," December 18, 2003.

Melissa Daly, "Clean Teens," *Current Health 2*, April–May 2005.

Laura D'Angelo, "Crushed Dreams," *Scholastic Scope*, March 22, 2004.

John DiConsiglio, "Generation Rx," *Choices*, December 2006.

Gary A. Enos, "Treatment Made Everything New," *Addiction Professional*, January–February 2006.

Geraldine Fabrikant, "From Wall Street to Mean Street," *New York Times*, August 24, 2003.

Thomas Fields-Meyer, Melinda Janiszewski, et al., "Over the Counter Killer: It's Cheap, It's Legal, and It's Available at Any Drugstore. DXM, a Cough Medicine Ingredient, Is the Latest Craze for Teens Who Want to Get High—or Die Trying," *People Weekly*, February 2, 2004.

Mike Kessler, "Dear Mom and Dad: Sorry, I Lied. (But You Knew That, Right?)," *Skiing*, December 2004.

Melissa Klein, "Rx for Trouble: Abusing Drugs Can Destroy Lives," *Current Health 1*, November 2005.

Know Your World Extra, "Free Again: This Teen Is Fighting Drug Addiction—and Getting His Life Back," November 3, 2006.

Julie Mehta, "Whiff of Trouble," *Current Health 2*, September 2006.

——— "Dark Crystal: Meet Three Young People Who Got Swept Up in Meth Madness," *Current Health 2*, November 2005.

Carole Moore, "The Yellow Brick Road to Nowhere: America's Youngest Drug Addicts," *Law Enforcement Technology*, September 2005.

Michelle Lee Ribeiro with Sarah Richards, "When Prescription Drugs Kill," *CosmoGIRL!*, March 2005.

Maria Rodale, "Best Meal of the Day," *Organic Style*, October 2004.

Patrick Rogers, "Prescription for Death: A Powerful Painkilling Pill Called OxyContin Brings Relief to Millions—and Suffering to a Small Pennsylvania Town," *People Weekly*, August 13, 2001.

Bonnie Miller Rubin, "High on Cold and Cough Medicine," *Good Housekeeping*, October 2005.

Larry S. Schlesinger, "Alcohol, Drugs, and a Residency," *Pediatric News*, January 2006.

Maggie Stone, as told to Louise Jarvis, "Dark Crystal," *Teen Vogue*, December 2005.

Alex Tresniowski, Kristin Harmel, and Lori Rozsa, "The Gun, the Son, and a Father's Love: To Save His Son from Ten Years in Prison, Danny Cummings Had to Risk His Own Life," *People Weekly*, May 9, 2005.

Internet Sources

Stephanie Armour, "Meth Abuse at Work Continues to Grow," *USA Today.com*, July 14, 2005. www.usatoday.com/money/workplace/2005-07-14-meth-usat_x.htm.

Cate Baily, "The Lows of Getting High: Alby's Story," National Institute for Drug Abuse, 2003. http://teens.drugabuse.gov/stories/story_mjl.asp.

Drugstory.org, "It All Started with Pot—An Interview with Lauren." www.drugstory.org/feature/lauren.asp.

Charlotte Sanders, "I Felt Like Super Mom," June 5, 2006. www.drugfree.org/Portal/Stories/I_Felt_Like_Super_Mom.

Lynn Smith, "Agony from Ecstasy" http://checkyourself.com/ShowRealStory.aspx?storyId= b0935c9d-aff4-4ae 5-93ee-752b1dc27026.

Index